Cryptic Crosswords for Beginners

By Amy Fisher

2022

Cryptic Crosswords for Beginners

Table of Contents

Written by Amy Fisher, 2022

Note: Most puzzles in this book do not follow standard rules for cryptic crossword layouts. These are intentionally much simpler and easier to help you learn each of the wordplay types. Many clues may not have smooth surface reading or use accurate definitions according to the dictionary. This book is for players, not constructors. :)

Cover Art - Created in Canva
Editors - Jon Fisher, Darren Miller, and Anne-Marie Tuck

Cryptic Clues Are Weird!

You're about to dive into the wild world of cryptic crosswords! These unique puzzles look quite strange at the start, especially if you have only ever played a regular crossword. But do not fear! This book will teach you how to read these complicated clues and give you plenty of examples to begin deciphering clues on your own.

Included: An overview on how to solve a cryptic clue, many lists of indicator words to help you know what kind of wordplay to look for, easy themed puzzles to help understand each type of wordplay, and medium-difficulty puzzles that incorporate everything you've learned!

My best tip for starting out is to look up the answers as you go. Obviously take a crack at the clue to begin, but if you're stumped, it's better to look it up in the back than to feel too frustrated. You'll get used to the formatting of the clues, and you might learn a new word! Eventually you'll be quicker at noticing the wordplay and recognizing common abbreviations. But when you begin, always look in the back. No shame in it!

Similarly to looking in the back, if you like trying your hand at popular cryptic crosswords like those in *The Guardian*, *The Independent*, *Inquisitor*, and others, you'll want to check out fifteensquared.net. This website helps you find the answers, as well as understand the wordplay. Just like looking in the back for answers, it is very helpful to learn the wordplay that the constructor uses to make their games. Never feel like you're cheating when you do this! It is all part of learning. The more you attempt cryptic crosswords and understand the answers, the better you'll be at solving them by yourself in the future.

But with this book in particular, I believe in you that you won't need the answer key at every turn. We'll start out slow, introducing each type of wordplay with plenty of examples. I encourage you to read (and play) this book in the order that it's presented. Also, we've included a HINTS page. Some puzzles won't be highlighted to show the wordplay sections, but you can find the highlighted version in the hints. Before you look up the answers on those puzzles, check the hints to see the different wordplay sections. You might be able to solve it by yourself at that point!

Alright, enough of this intro! Let's get started with learning cryptic crosswords. :)

Crossword Terminology and Basics

Here are some terms you'll need to learn before we start on crosswords.

- <u>Grid</u> - The diagram of black and white squares where words will connect.
- <u>Across Word</u> - Words that will be written across, or horizontally, like you normally read words.
- <u>Down Word</u> - Words that will be written down, or vertically. Start the word at the top and write the letters below each other.
- <u>White Square</u> - These are for writing in letters to solve the crossword.
- <u>Black Square</u> - These are blocks to show you where a word stops.
- <u>Clue Number</u> - Where you should enter the word you solved. Sometimes you have the same clue number for an Across clue and a Down clue. These will share the same starting letter, but be written in different directions.
  Ex. Kazoo is 1 Across & Knife is 1 Down
- <u>Unchecked Square</u> - A square where you have a single word to help you solve it. No other clues will 'check' your answer for these squares.
- <u>Checked Square</u> - A square that is 'checked' by another clue. If you are unsure of your answer, you have another clue to verify if that letter is correct or not. Ex. 12 Across is a completely checked clue!

- <u>Constructor</u> - The person that creates the board, fills it with connecting words and writes clever clues. This person might also set a theme for the puzzle. In other countries, this person might be called the compiler or setter.
- <u>Symmetry</u> - A typical feature in crosswords where you can spin the board 180 degrees and the black squares are in the same places.
- <u>Word Count or Enumeration</u> - The number of letters in the final answer. Any important punctuation will be notated as well. If an answer is more than one word, it will be marked in the enumeration by a comma. Ex. DINOSAUR has enumeration (8), MOTHERINLAW has enumeration (6-2-3), THANKYOU has enumeration (5,3)

Your First Cryptic Crossword

Here's your typical cryptic crossword. Don't worry if this looks daunting! They are complicated for everyone at first. At the end of this manual, you'll come back to this puzzle and find that you understand the clues with your new-found knowledge. You're more than capable of solving these puzzles with a bit of practice. So take a gander and move on to the next page!

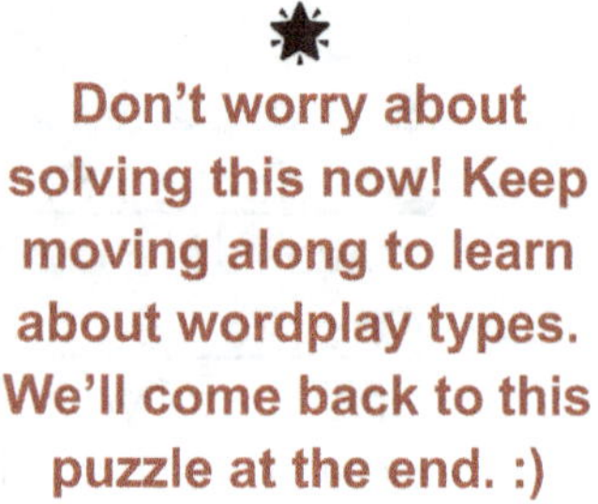

Don't worry about solving this now! Keep moving along to learn about wordplay types. We'll come back to this puzzle at the end. :)

	ACROSS				DOWN		
1	Power source found in faux eel, oddly (4)	13	Fruit with tulip core is a valuable item (5)	1	Bewilder mist (3)	11	Circle part of Bob or Derek (6)
3	Sorority leader tags male deer (5)	16	Period of time sounds like yours and mine (3)	2	Attorney returned real Wyoming stuffing (6)	12	Half of plainest home (4)
6	Glare from exhausted general with a cry of pain (4)	17	Go inside any affliction (5)	3	Small lime ooze (5)	13	Illegally hunt quiet Oscar at empty athletic hospital (5)
8	Popular key with English coordinate! (5)	18	Ta-da, corrected information (4)	4	Hearing gold God from Italy (5)	14	Float around in the air (5)
9	Tuber month making a come back (3)	20	Furious with the Spanish inn (5)	5	Three score and nine Romans stuck in pigpen (5)	15	Play old segment back true (5)
10	Box of nuts originally filled every case of dark wood (5)	21	Bridge monster dropped tea to spin (4)	7	Path created by Louisiana and Nebraska (4)	19	Entire mall won't start (3)

<u>Overview</u>

Cryptic crosswords are very different from regular crosswords. You cannot read a cryptic crossword clue like you would a regular clue.

Look at this example:

Regular clue:	`Animal that says "Meow" (3)`	Answer: Cat
Cryptic clue:	`Animal hiding in location (3)`	Answer: Cat

There are two parts to a cryptic clue. The STRAIGHT part and the <u>WORDPLAY</u> part. The STRAIGHT part gives you the definition of the word, though sometimes vaguely. The <u>WORDPLAY</u> part is more complicated, and that is what this book will focus on most.

In the clue above, the STRAIGHT part is the beginning: Animal. The WORDPLAY part is the end: <u>hiding in location</u>.

Now, this doesn't mean an actual animal hiding in a random location. The word 'hiding' means the answer we need is hiding inside the word 'location'!

L O <u>C A T</u> I O N

Do you see it now?

There are many ways to use wordplay to create cryptic clues! You can use **Anagrams, Homophones, Additions, Deletions, Hidden Words, Double Definition, Charades,** and many more! We'll go over each type of clue on later pages.

⭐ <u>The key to solving a cryptic crossword is to NOT read the sentence as it is given. It's unlikely that the sentence will make much sense, and even more unlikely to give a reasonable answer.</u>

The first step to solving these is to separate the STRAIGHT part from the <u>WORDPLAY</u> part. The straight clue will ALWAYS be at the beginning or end of the clue, never in the middle!

Cryptic Clue	Answer	Explanation
Change <u>in Damendorf</u> (5)	AMEND	The word 'amend' is inside the word D<u>amend</u>orf
<u>Part of strawberry</u> isn't cooked (3)	RAW	The word 'raw' is part of the word st<u>raw</u>berry
<u>Lethal venom secretly split in two</u> (5)	HALVE	The word 'halve' is at the end of 'Let<u>hal</u>' and the beginning of '<u>ve</u>nom'. This clue is shared between the two first words!

Hidden Word Clues

Hidden Word clues are some of the easier types of clues to decipher. Hidden Word clues will literally hide the answer within other words in the clue!

The way you can tell if something is a Hidden Word clue is by looking for the INDICATOR word.

Here's a list of some common Hidden Word Indicators:

HIDDEN WORD INDICATORS

Appears in	Buried in	Camouflages	Concealed by	Contained in	Dwells in
Extract	Fragment	From	Held by	Hidden in	In
Inside	Part	Partial	Piece of	Sample	Secretly
Selection	Shackled by	Some	Stores	Stuffing	Within

*This list is not exhaustive! There are many other ways that puzzle-makers will indicate a hidden word, but this list is a good start to recognizing them.

Examples:

The straight clue is in blue. The wordplay is underlined.
The indicator is in light green.

Cryptic Clue	Answer	Explanation
Change in Damendorf (5)	AMEND	The word 'amend' is inside the word Damendorf
Part of strawberry isn't cooked (3)	RAW	The word 'raw' is part of the word strawberry
Lethal venom secretly split in two (5)	HALVE	The word 'halve' is at the end of 'Lethal' and the beginning of 'venom'. This clue is shared between the two first words!
Short water predator lurks in epic rocks (4)	CROC	Croc is the shortened form of Crocodile. It's hidden between the words 'epic' and 'rocks".
Road appears in planet (4)	LANE	The word 'lane' appears in the word planet
Fragment of Earth, I eventually steal (6)	THIEVE	The word 'thieve' is split between 3 words: 'Earth, I eventually'. The comma can be ignored.

Reversal Clues

Reversal clues tell you to flip a word backwards, or to seek out a backwards clue that is hidden. For now, we'll start out with reversed hidden words, but these indicators will come into play more later in this book.

The way you can tell if something is a Reversed clue is by looking for the INDICATOR word.

Here's a list of some common Reversal Indicators:

REVERSAL INDICATORS

For Across Clues	About face	Back up	Comeback	Flip	Go west	In return
	Invert	Reflect-ive	Retro	Reverse	Somer-sault	Wrong way
For Down Clues	Ascend	Fall over	Heading north	Lift	On the rise	Put up
	Send up	Tip	Upend	Upstand-ing	Upturned	Write up

*This list is not exhaustive! There are many other ways that puzzle-makers will indicate a reversed word, but this list is a good start to recognizing them.

Oftentimes these clues are combined with Hidden Word clues, so you will see both indicators to let you know it is hidden and backwards.

Examples:

The straight clue is in blue. The wordplay is underlined.
The hidden indicator is in light green, and the reversal indicator is in dark green.

Cryptic Clue	Answer	Explanation
Tent stake holds large possums back (3)	PEG	The word 'peg' is backwards in the words 'large possums'
Eyre stores retro bread (3)	RYE	The word 'rye' is backwards in the name "Eyre"
Drink with no jump faced backwards (5)	DECAF	The word 'decaf' is the word 'faced' backwards. No hidden clue this time!
Assemble part of camera per particular set up (7)	PREPARE	The word 'prepare' is hidden backwards in the words 'camera per particular'

Christmas Cryptic (Hidden Word Clues - Highlighted)

In this cryptic crossword, all answers are Christmas-related words. Also, all clues use the hidden word wordplay format only. Some words will be hidden forwards, and some will be backwards. The sections of the clue are highlighted for you. The straight part is in blue, and the hidden word indicator(s) are in green. Good luck!

Answers on pg 57

	ACROSS		DOWN
3	Tree color sample comes back as engineer grows (5)	1	Rancid eraser contains apple beverage (5)
5	Church song contributing to sin; my hope overthrown (4)	2	Unusual cat nastiness in return from gift giver (5,5)
7	Secretly brought in select foil decoration (6)	4	Section of flipped fish plod urgently for red-nosed reindeer (7)
9	Cougar landed inside wreath (7)	6	There's no way prisoners make the ground white (4)
10	Santa's helper factors in welfare (3)	8	Dugong gets portion of recalled holiday drink (6)
11	Praise crew or shipmate partially (7)	12	Fragment of mustardy tree-topper (4)

US President Cryptic (Hidden Word Clues)

In this cryptic crossword, all answers are US President's last names. Also, all clues use the hidden word wordplay format only. Some words will be hidden forwards, and some will be backwards. The sections of the clue are not highlighted for you this time. Good luck!

Hints on pg 49, Answers on pg 57

	ACROSS		DOWN
3	Seventh president partly hijacks onlookers (7)	1	No sir, Rahab attributes overturning to ninth president (8)
5	First president conceals brainwashing tongue (10)	2	Mice or no mice? Some back the fifth president (6)
8	38th president is partly affordable (4)	4	Nomad is on displays as fourth president (7)
9	27th president is buried in hot fat rearwards (4)	6	Peg ran towards content of 18th president (5)
11	20th president dwells in sugar fields (8)	7	Some psycho overreacts to 31st president (6)
12	Component of plush Subaru recalled for 43rd president (4)	10	Plasma dances upright secretly for the second president (5)

Anagram Clues

Anagram clues are another easier type of clue to decipher. Anagram clues will have all the letters of the answer in the clue, but rearranged!

For example: STALE/LEAST/TALES are all anagrams of each other. They use the same letters, but in different orders.

Here's a list of some common Anagram Indicators:

ANAGRAM INDICATORS

Altered	Badly	Complicated	Crazy	Different	Fractured
Funny	Jumbled	Kind of	Loosely	Messy	Naughty
New	Not Right	Ordered	Organized	Out	Possibly
Reform	Roughly	Ruined	Sad	Shifting	Sloppy
Spoil	Transform	Turning	Variation	Wild	Wrongly

*This list is not exhaustive! There are many other ways that puzzle-makers will indicate an anagrammed word, but this list is a good start to recognizing them.

Examples:

The straight clue is in blue. The wordplay is underlined. The indicator is in orange.

Cryptic Clue	Answer	Explanation
Deformed tulip smoked (3,2)	LIT UP	'Lit up' is an anagram of the word 'tulip'
Go mad about belief (5)	DOGMA	'Dogma' is an anagram of the words 'go mad'
Inspirational conversation kept pal organized (3,4)	PEP TALK	'Pep talk' is an anagram of the words 'kept pal'
Bike and yen screw up chili ingredient (6,4)	KIDNEY BEAN	'Kidney Bean' is an anagram of the words 'bike and yen'
Morals broke a slide (6)	IDEALS	'Ideals' is an anagram of the words 'a slide'
Anna ruined Indian food (4)	NAAN	'Naan' is an anagram of the name 'Anna'

Clothing Cryptic (Anagram Clues - Highlighted)

In this cryptic crossword, all answers are clothing items. Also, all clues use the anagram wordplay format only. The sections of the clue are highlighted for you. The straight part is in blue, and the anagram word indicator is in orange. Good luck!

Answers on pg 58

	ACROSS		DOWN
2	Orca ain't moving for a weatherproof jacket (8)	1	Hand warmers are freely smitten (7)
4	Fancy top is so blue; not right (6)	3	A fancy tie made from tacos (5)
6	A cot potentially helps in a storm (4)	4	Wrap both bare somehow (8)
7	Bananas are west and could be ugly (7)	5	Hoses modified for your feet (5)
10	Surprising bar supports the girls (3)	6	Open cover for messy arcading (8)
11	Wrongly jam a spa for nightwear (7)	8	Lenses curiously sag less (7)
12	Men's undergarments rob sex; kinky (6)	9	Denim, as Jen ordered (5)

Mythical Creature Cryptic (Anagram Clues)

In this cryptic crossword, all answers are mythical creatures. Also, all clues use the anagram wordplay format only. The sections of the clue are not highlighted for you this time. Good luck!

Hints on pg 50, Answers on pg 58

	ACROSS		DOWN
6	A peer lunch may be found on St. Patrick's Day (10)	1	Correctly uncrate half-man half-horse (7)
9	Flaming bird mishandles oxen hip (7)	2	Drunkenly nag Rod for giant reptile (6)
10	Cook me a rich Greek monster (7)	3	I revamp strange blood-sucker (7)
12	Gore turned into a green monster (4)	4	Fantastic horse may incur no corruption (7)
13	I fry a naughty pixie (5)	5	Gene, I could be one who grants wishes (5)
14	I tye badly for an abominable snowman (4)	7	Disguise gem on garden creature (5)
15	Sh, got wild spirit? (5)	8	Flying horse has Pa guess loosely (7)
16	Awful tumor in a bullish man (8)	11	Mischievous creature rambles in blog (6)

Weather Cryptic (Review - Highlighted)

In this cryptic crossword, all answers are weather-related words. Also, all clues use either hidden word or anagram format. The sections of the clue are highlighted for you. The straight part is in blue, the hidden word indicators are in green and the anagram indicators are in orange. Good luck!

Answers on pg 59

	ACROSS		DOWN
4	Mort's design creates violent weather (5)	1	Light rain disfigures crate (5)
8	Nightlight disguised centaur or alpaca (6)	2	Silly ape's mother envelopes the planet (10)
9	Okra in bowl provides many colors (7)	3	Eve, what a grotesque hot-spell! (8)
10	Center of hurricane buried in grey earth (3)	5	Ms., it developed dew (4)
12	Bow onstage features returning ice crystals (4)	6	Frantically misroute wetness (8)
13	Turbulent sorrow in dystopian content (5)	7	Recover castle concealing cloudiness (8)
14	Mature Peter troubled by hot and cold (11)	11	Vortex demolished donator (7)
15	Disturbing noise from smooth underwear (7)	12	Risk your content for something to look up to (3)

Fruit Cryptic (Review)

In this cryptic crossword, all answers are fruit. Also, all clues use either the hidden word wordplay, or the anagram wordplay format. The sections of the clue are not highlighted for you. Good luck!

Hints on pg 50, Answers on pg 59

	ACROSS		DOWN
3	Fruit has curious lump (4)	1	Fruit found in panda tent (4)
6	Giftwrap ricotta inside fruit (7)	2	Nope. Actual trouble is fruit (10)
8	Fruit interfered with mile (4)	3	Hippo, Meg, ran at Evelyn hiding fruit (11)
10	Reap unusual fruit (4)	4	Letters from Cuban; a natural fruit (6)
11	An ogre jumbled fruit (6)	5	Khaki wizard disguises fruit (4)
12	Piece of fungiform reversed fruit (3)	7	Fruit ruined pagers (6)
13	Wildly cheap fruit (5)	9	Fruit demonstrates human goals (5)

Homophone Clues

Homophone clues use how a word or phrase sounds to help you solve it. Words like THERE/THEIR/THEY'RE are homophones of each other.

Here's a list of some common Homophone Indicators:

HOMOPHONE INDICATORS

Aloud	Announced	Audibly	Broadcast	By the sound of it	Called out
Expressed	For the listener	Heard	In conversation	Listen	On the radio
Overheard	Reported	Said	Sound	Spoken	Verbally

Examples:

The straight clue is in blue. The wordplay is underlined. The indicator is in purple.

Cryptic Clue	Answer	Explanation
Sunrise announced grief (8)	MOURNING	We need a homophone of sunrise that means **grief**. In this case, the word is MORNING, which sounds like MOURNING. The second word is correct because it has 8 letters, as the enumeration says.
Surcharge on pushpins, say. (3)	TAX	Homophone of pushpins that means **surcharge**. In this case, the pushpins mean TACKS, sounding like TAX.
I heard an aircraft is boring (6)	PLAIN	Homophone of aircraft that means **boring**. For this, you find PLANE, sounding like PLAIN.

Another verbal kind of clue is called **Spoonerisms**. This is where you switch the initial sounds of two words or syllables. (credited to Reverend Spooner)

Ex. Daisy Lay = Lazy Day, Belly Jeans = Jelly Beans, Cheater = Teacher

These clues will always include the name Spooner or Reverend as an indicator.

Cryptic Clue	Answer	Explanation
Spooner yells "Die spur!" to a creepy crawly (6)	SPIDER	Spoonerism clues switch the first sounds of two words. If you switch the D and Sp, you get SPIDER, a creepy crawly
Reverend announces fun cues that baffle (7)	CONFUSE	Switch the F and C sounds to get 'confuse', which means baffle

Food Cryptic (Homophone Clues - Highlighted)

In this cryptic crossword, all answers are food items. Also, all clues use homophone wordplay format only. The sections of the clue are highlighted for you. The straight part is in blue, and the homophone word indicator is in purple. Good luck!

Answers on pg 60

	ACROSS		DOWN
4	Audibly entomb fruit (5)	1	Circle constant read aloud for dessert (3)
5	Spooner says "Beat mall for spaghetti topping" (8)	2	Spice is measured by clocks, reportedly (5)
6	Whipped chocolate dessert sounds like large deer (6)	3	Frozen dessert for boar, say, from the Reverend (6)
8	"Defeated!" announced round veggie (4)	4	Ghost noises over the radio for alcohol (5)
11	Taster told of distilled alcohol (6)	7	Pepper is cold, by the sound of it (5)
12	Diamond measurement overheard as orange vegetable (6)	8	Roll reproduced audibly (5)
13	Vocally complain for white or red (4)	9	Golf assistant called out for hot drink (3)
14	Repeated offender spoke of breakfast food (6)	10	Officer announced popcorn piece (6)

Types of People Cryptic (Homophone Clues)

In this cryptic crossword, all answers are occupations or types of people. Also, all clues use homophone wordplay format only. The sections of the clue are not highlighted for you. Good luck!

Hints on pg 51, Answers on pg 60

	ACROSS		DOWN
1	Spooner asks, "Say, men lay bricks?" (5)	2	Nothing on the radio, sister (3)
3	Uncle's wife sounds like tiny insect (4)	4	Private teacher is a person who plays the horn audibly (5)
6	Nobleman overheard evening darkness (6)	5	"Hem clothes later." says the Reverend (6)
9	Ranked official is related to war, by the sound of it (7)	7	Drug mumbled to female hero (7)
11	Poet is not allowed to enter hearing (4)	8	"Make money!", announced oracle (7)
14	School head told fundamental truth (9)	10	Person in sales reported basement (6)
15	Candy packaging in audition as spoken word musician (6)	12	Asking for specifying information outloud for enchantress (5)
16	I heard broiler is a religious monk (5)	13	Broadcast decorative knot for lover boy (4)

Body Parts Cryptic (Review - Highlighted)

In this cryptic crossword, all answers are body parts. Also, all clues use either hidden word, anagram or homophone wordplay format. The sections of the clue are highlighted for you. The straight part is in blue, the hidden word indicators are in green, the anagram indicators are in orange, and the homophone word indicators are in purple. Good luck!

Answers on pg 61

	ACROSS		DOWN
3	Uh, Tom? Messy pie hole (5)	1	Smelling device is aware, reportedly (4)
5	Pastel knapsacks secretly comeback for foot joint (5)	2	The E.T. fractured pearly whites (5)
8	Yeah, I psychotically conceal hindquarters (4)	4	Midsection is trash, by the sound of it (5)
9	Ticker reformed Earth (5)	6	Sternum contains cliche standards (5)
11	Futon guest held by licker (6)	7	Digester wrongly shot Cam (7)
13	Wild rabbit spoke of head fur (4)	10	Ram organized an appendage (3)
14	Book needs part of patella (4)	12	Belly button is related to the Navy, verbally (5)

Countries Cryptic (Review)

In this cryptic crossword, all answers are names of countries. Also, all clues use either hidden word, anagram or homophone wordplay format. The sections of the clue are not highlighted for you. Good luck!

Hints on pg 51, Answers on pg 61

	ACROSS		DOWN
1	Partially kidnap a jaguar. Bring back to Asian island country (5)	1	Acai jam ordered from Caribbean country (7)
3	Dairy store dwells back in Middle Eastern country (5)	2	South American country is kind of pure (4)
4	Funny aroma in European country (7)	6	Rebel, I zest secretly for Caribbean country (6)
5	Glitch in atoms conceal rich country (5)	8	Type 'G' randomly for pharaoh's home (5)
7	Balkan country reported oily substance (6)	9	Mediterranean island listens to evergreen tree (6)
10	Nairobi's country hidden in broken yacht (5)	10	Spooner says, "Woo Kate in the Middle East" (6)
12	Aga, our quiet alien, transformed west African country (10,6)	11	Ringwald heard landlocked African country (4)

Common Abbreviations

Abbreviations are VERY common in cryptic crosswords. Crossword makers utilize many types of abbreviations including states, countries, elements, directions, scientific constants and many more. Here are several lists to get you started. There are plenty more than what I've listed, so be open to learning as you go. :)

US States - you might also see the word 'state' to mean any of these abbreviations

Alabama	AL	Alaska	AK	Arizona	AZ	Arkansas	AR	California	CA
Colorado	CO	Connecticut	CT	Delaware	DE	Florida	FL	Georgia	GA
Hawaii	HI	Idaho	ID	Illinois	IL	Indiana	IN	Iowa	IA
Kansas	KS	Kentucky	KY	Louisiana	LA	Maine	ME	Maryland	MD
Massachusetts	MA	Michigan	MI	Minnesota	MN	Mississippi	MS	Missouri	MO
Montana	MT	Nebraska	NE	Nevada	NV	New Hampshire	NH	New Jersey	NJ
New Mexico	NM	New York	NY	North Carolina	NC	North Dakota	ND	Ohio	OH
Oklahoma	OK	Oregon	OR	Pennsylvania	PA	Rhode Island	RI	South Carolina	SC
South Dakota	SD	Tennessee	TN	Texas	TX	Utah	UT	Vermont	VT
Virginia	VA	Washington	WA	West Virginia	WV	Wisconsin	WI	Wyoming	WY

NATO Alphabet

Alpha	A	Bravo	B	Charlie	C	Delta	D	Echo	E	Foxtrot	F	Golf	G
Hotel	H	India	I	Juliet	J	Kilo	K	Lima	L	Mike	M	November	N
Oscar	O	Papa	P	Quebec	Q	Romeo	R	Sierra	S	Tango	T	Uniform	U
		Victor	V	Whiskey	W	X-ray	X	Yankee	Y	Zulu	Z		

Common Chemical Abbreviations

Hydrogen	H	Helium	HE	Boron	B	Carbon	C	Iron	FE
Nitrogen	N	Oxygen	O	Fluorine	F	Potassium	K	Tungsten	W
Phosphorous	P	Uranium	U	Sodium	NA	Gold	AU	Silver	AG

Common Country Abbreviations

Austria	A, AU	Belgium	B, BE	Switzerland	CH	China	CN	Germany	D, DE
Spain	E, ES	France	F, FR	Gabon	G, GA	Liechtenstein	FL	Hungary	H, HU
Italy	I, IT	Japan	J, JP	Luxembourg	L, LUX	Malta	M, MT	Norway	N, NO
Portugal	P, PT	Indonesia	RI, ID	Sweden	S, SE	Thailand	T, TH	U.S. of A.	US

Common One-Letter Abbreviations

Acceleration, Ace, Adult, Alto, Ampere, Great Grade	A	Bass, Born, Bye, Byte, Good Grade	B
Celsius, Cent, Clubs, Cold, Copyright, Hundred	C	Day, Daughter, Democrat, Density, Diameter	D
Earth, East, Energy, European	E	Fahrenheit, False, Female, Fine, Forte	F
Gallon, German, Good, Gram, Grand	G	Height, Hearts, Hospital, Hot, Hour, Husband	H
Independent, International, Island, One	I	Energy, Jack, Judge	J
Kelvin, Kilo, King	K	Fifty, Lake, Large, Left, Length, Liberal, Student	L
Male, Married, Mass, Medium, Mile, Minute, Month	M	New, Newton, Number, North, Noun	N
Egg, Hug, Love, Nothing, Old, Please, Ring, Zero	O	Page, Parking, Piano, Per, Power, Pressure	P
Quarter, Queen, Question	Q	Radius, Republican, Right, River, Run	R
Second, Singular, Small, Soprano, South, Spades,	S	Tenor, Tense, Time, Ton, True	T
Unionist, United, University	U	Five, Velocity, Verb, Very, Victory, Volt	V
Watt, Weight, West, Width, Wife, With	W	By, Kiss, Unknown, Times, Ten, Variable, Vote	X
Club, Year, Yes	Y	Last, Sound of Sleep, Ultimate, Zero	Z

Homophone One-Letter Abbreviations

A	A	Be, Bee	B	See, Sea	C	Gee	G	Aye, Eye, I	I
Jay	J	Kay	K	Oh, Owe	O	Pee, Pea	P	Cue, Queue	Q
Are	R	Tea, Tee	T	Ewe, You	U	Ex	X	Why	Y

Common Two-Letter Abbreviations

Afternoon	PM	Afterthought	PS	Alien	ET	America	US
Artillery	RA	At Home, Popular	IN	Attorney	DA	British	BR
Business	CO	Catholic	RC	City	NY,LA	Commercial	AD
Computers	IT,PC	Constant	PI	Copy	CC	Disease	TB,ME
Doctor	DR,MB,GP	Electricity	AC,DC	Exercise	PE	Father	FR
Example	EG	Graduate	BA,MA	Gun	AK,BB	Host	MC
Investigator	PI	Loudspeaker	PA	Morning	AM	Nazis	SS
Northeast	NE	Northwest	NW	Now	AD	Old City	UR
Papers	ID	Pencil	HB	Pound	LB	Queen	HM,ER
Record	CD,EP,LP	Sailor	AB,OS,PO	Saint/Street	ST	Setter	ME
Soldier	GI,RM,RE	Southeast	SE	Southwest	SW	That is	IE
Toilet	WC	Very Loud	FF	Very Quiet	PP	Work	PO

Roman numerals are common, and not just the single uses of I, V, X, and so on. You might see the word 'six' used as VI, or 'fifty-four' as LIV.

Months and days of the week can also be abbreviated! JAN, FEB... MON, TUE... etc.

Some advanced cryptic crossword clues will use words that could mean several different abbreviation options:

'Direction' could mean north, south, east or west! So you'd replace it with either N, S, E or W. The same is true for words like 'bearing', 'heading', 'point', 'quarter'.

The word 'note' is commonly used to mean musical note. Unfortunately, this has many different abbreviation possibilities, too!
'Note' or 'Key' could refer to simply the letters used in music, (A B C D E F or G)
'Note' could also refer to the solfege terms we give to music notes (DO RE MI FA SO LA or TI)

Basically, if you ever see the word 'note' in a clue, be careful!

Smaller words from various languages might make an appearance in your cryptic clues. 'Article' might refer to the word A, AN, or THE. 'The' in Spanish is EL, LA, LAS, or LOS. 'The' in French is DU or LE. 'The' in German is DER, DAS, or DIE. 'The' in Italian is IL.

Abbreviations are very common in cryptic crosswords! One of the best sites to research even more abbreviations is crackingcrosswords.co.uk.

Examples:

The straight clue is in blue. Abbreviations are pink. The wordplay is underlined.

Cryptic Clue	Answer	Explanation
Praise good grade less (5)	BLESS	Good grade, in this case, stands for B. B + LESS = BLESS
Florida silver mark (4)	FLAG	Florida stands for FL, and silver stands for AG. FL + AG = FLAG
Father, why cook with oil? (3)	FRY	Father is FR, and why stands for the letter Y. FR + Y = FRY
Three notes cease to work (6)	RETIRE	Three notes, in this case, refers to RE, TI, and RE. RE + TI + RE = RETIRE
Stan, the German onlooker (7)	STANDER	'The' in German could be DER STAN + DER = STANDER

Addition & Deletion Indicators

Addition and Deletion indicators help you know if you are supposed to add or take away something. This can be a whole word or just a few letters. Abbreviations are often included in these types of clues. Additions can also be called Containers, especially when you add one word inside of another.

Here's a list of some common Addition and Deletion Indicators:

ADDITION/CONTAINER INDICATORS

Simple addition	And	By	Joins	Next to	On	With
Somewhere in the middle	Around	Between	Captures	Held	Inside	Protects

DELETION INDICATORS

Simple Deletion	Abandons	Brushing off	Chucked	Cut	Deprived of	Disowning
	Ditched	Eliminated	Fired	Ignored	No/Not	Shed
Remove first letter	Behead	Cap off	First cut	Lead away	Not starting	Topless
Remove last letter	Almost	Curtail	Footloose	Mostly	Not Quite	Short

The straight clue is in blue. The wordplay is <u>underlined.</u> The indicator is in yellow.

Cryptic Clue	Answer	Explanation
Loud music protects tuna, very lucky (9)	FORTUNATE	Add the word 'tuna' to the inside of the word 'forte' meaning loud music. FORTUNATE
Web address is neutral, not neat (1.1.1)	URL	Delete the letters 'neat' from the word 'neutral', you are left with just the u,r, and l. URL is an initialism, so it is notated as (1.1.1) instead of (3)
Stair missing a whisk (4)	STIR	Delete the letter 'a' from 'stair', you are left with 'stir'
Put corgi in so Papa can replace golf sign (7)	SCORPIO	'Corgi' inside 'so' = Scorgio, Papa (P) replaces Golf (G) SCORGIO + P - G = SCORPIO
Thug loses head from embrace (3)	HUG	Remove the head (first letter) of 'thug' to get 'hug'

Animal Cryptic (Abbreviations - Highlighted)

In this cryptic crossword, all answers are animals. Also, all clues use additions, deletions, and many abbreviations. The sections of the clue are highlighted for you. The straight clue is in blue, additions are light yellow, deletions are dark yellow, and abbreviations are pink. Good luck!

Answers on pg 62

	ACROSS		DOWN
2	Endless cowl is dairy animal (3)	1	She joins record as wooly mammal (5)
5	Reptile wizard replaces wife with $50 (6)	2	Inch inside; chill next to a gray rodent (10)
6	Beer captures a victory for dam maker (6)	3	Toad from fog surrounding river (4)
8	Slot joins hospital; it's a deadly sin! (5)	4	Deceitful person puts whiskey on easel (6)
10	Dromedary browned sugar; fired artillery (5)	7	King swallowed by money becomes primate (6)
12	Pack animal lam inside Los Angeles (5)	9	Bath, not hot, for flying mammal (3)
13	Pinniped comes from southeast Alabama (4)	11	Ostrich earmuffs block out very loud Arkansas soprano (3)

Round Things Cryptic (Abbreviations)

In this cryptic crossword, all answers are round things. Also, all clues use additions, deletions, and many abbreviations. The sections of the clue are not highlighted for you. Good luck!

Hints on pg 52, Answers on pg 62

	ACROSS		DOWN
4	One small boy in free flying saucer (7)	**1**	Tango or till a burrito staple (8)
6	See lock tell time (5)	**2**	Remove senior from shrub, find center of wheel (3)
7	South Africa has two notes about sandwich meat (6)	**3**	Gourd from Maine left nothing new (5)
8	Bag the Spanish breakfast roll (5)	**5**	Loud instrument is going without iodine (4)
10	Pressure Earl to form within an oyster (5)	**9**	Fruit of oak tree is alpha corn (5)
12	Four within ole martini garnish (5)	**10**	Pen by New York is one cent (5)
13	Moron ignored right, like Io or Titan (4)	**11**	Brings guillotine for marriage symbols (5)

Items in Your Pocket Cryptic (Abbreviations Review - Highlighted)

In this cryptic crossword, all answers are things you might find in your pocket. The sections of the clue are highlighted for you. The straight part is in blue, the hidden word indicators are in green, reversal indicators are in dark green, the anagram indicators are in orange, the homophone word indicators are in purple, the additions are light yellow, deletions are dark yellow, and abbreviations are pink. Good luck!

Answers on pg 63

	ACROSS		DOWN
4	Call or page hospital '1' (5)	1	Took pitch roughly and removes food (9)
5	See Andy? Sweets! (5)	2	Money in hidden storage, reportedly (4)
6	Pinkeye extract is very important (3)	3	Treatment cleaned up nice dime (8)
8	Fire starter concealed by twilight, erased (7)	7	Billfold is all wet on the outside (6)
12	Meant for throwing advice without a five (4)	9	Flipped mug possibly found under a desk (3)
13	Wrongly bill Pam for soothing dryness (3,4)	10	Junk buried in extra shack (5)
14	Chef and hiker alter cotton square (12)	11	Re-seat listener, acknowledging payment (7)
15	Father protects Earth from plumage (7)	14	Sounds like total depression (4)

Bugs Cryptic (Abbreviations Review)

In this cryptic crossword, all answers are bugs. Also, all clues use a combination of hidden words, reversals, anagrams, homophones, additions, deletions, and abbreviations. The sections of the clue are not highlighted for you. Good luck!

Hints on pg 52, Answers on pg 63

	ACROSS		DOWN
2	Tiny insect pant initially rejected (3)	1	Month, not November, loves the light (4)
5	Messy rags he props for flighty bug (11)	3	Fly can't set sermon secretly (6)
6	Graph identified hidden plantsucker (5)	4	Belgium alien left Earth for pest (6)
7	Flighty bug clouts roughly (6)	5	Tiny insect sends up tang (4)
10	Audibly run away from small insect (4)	8	CIA imprisons California democrat who makes loud buzzing noises (6)
11	Crazy spy marinating with holy bug? (7,6)	9	Sail captures new slimy mollusk (5)
13	I see inside the French head bugs (4)	12	Bloodsucking creature has habitual movement, reportedly (4)

Bits & Pieces Clues

Bits and Pieces clues take pieces of other words to either add or subtract to make new words. Most of the first letter and last letter indicators give a single letter, but sometimes they give more!

Ex. Capital of Denmark = D, Butt of joke = E, Heartless man = MN, Core of belief = LI

Here's a list of some common Bits and Pieces Indicators:

FIRST LETTER INDICATORS

At first	Bit of	Capital of	Early sign of	First in/of/to	Head of
Initially	Opening for/in/of	Original	Pinch of	Starter of	To begin with

LAST LETTER INDICATORS

At last	Butt of	Close to	Conclusion of	End of	Extreme of
Final	Finish of/off/to	Lastly	Tail of	Ultimately	What winds up

FIRST & LAST LETTERS INDICATORS

At the edges	Borders of	Cleared out	Extremes of	Gutless	Heartless
Hollow	Limits of/to	Outside	Shell of	Skin of	Wings of

MIDDLE LETTER INDICATORS

Belly of	Core of	Crux of	Essential ingredient	Heart of	Middle of

The straight clue is in blue. The wordplay is underlined. B&P indicator is in red.

Cryptic Clue	Answer	Explanation
Unnecessary sewing tools with pinch of steel (8)	NEEDLESS	Sewing tools here means NEEDLES. Pinch of steel is the first letter, S. NEEDLES + S = NEEDLESS
Crux of chemistry on charged atom (3)	ION	Crux, or center, of the word chemistry is the letter I. I + ON = ION
Trees bordering Oklahoma and Kansas (4)	OAKS	The borders, outside letters, of Oklahoma are OA, and Kansas are KS. OA + KS = OAKS

Letter Sequence Clues

Letter Sequence clues are similar to Bits and Pieces clues, except you will likely find more than a few letters hidden this way, either spread out regularly throughout the clue, or through some other pattern that will be indicated to you.

Here's a list of some common Letter Sequence Indicators:

ACROSTIC INDICATORS

Beginners	Firstly	For Starters	Heads	Initially	Leads

SELECT LETTER INDICATORS

Alternately	Evenly	Every other	Oddly	Odds	Regularly

DROP LETTER INDICATORS

Evens out	Not even	Nothing odd	Oddly lacking	Regular losses	Seconds out

OTHER PATTERN INDICATORS

Ends of	Tails	Edges of	Heads off	Initially away	Centrally

Examples:
The straight clue is in blue. The wordplay is underlined. Sequence indicator is in teal.

Cryptic Clue	Answer	Explanation
Oddly, counties are clever (4)	CUTE	The odd letters of 'CoUnTiEs' spell 'cute'.
Change of direction leads to zero issues globally (3)	ZIG	The leading letters of 'zero issues globally' spells the word 'zig'
Manx got feet removed by tropical fruit (5)	MANGO	When you remove the feet (last letters) of Manx and got, you are left with Man and go. Mango!
Bar starts renting out drinks (3)	ROD	The starting letters of 'renting out drinks' spells the word 'rod'
Half of diners crash (3)	DIN	Half of the word 'diners' is 'din', which is a loud noise, like a crash.

Boys Names Cryptic (B&P & Letter Sequence Clues - Highlighted)

In this cryptic crossword, all answers are popular boys' names. Also, all clues use bits and pieces clues or letter sequence clues. The sections of the clue are highlighted for you. The straight part is in blue, the bits and pieces indicators are in red, and the letter sequence indicators are in teal. Good luck!

Answers on pg 64

	ACROSS		DOWN
1	Empty bottle with bit of nectarine for Affleck (3)	1	Country singer Shelton is head of Branson lake (5)
3	Inventor Newton evenly rigs balance (5)	2	Tyson cleared out milkshake (4)
4	Spielberg at heart of Boston even (6)	4	Mr. Bean from sea close to Spain (4)
7	First man at edges of armed asylum (4)	5	Niche of last tailless Jonas brother (8)
8	Nicholson leads Joe around clean kitchen (4)	6	Odd plant for Wheel of Fortune host (3)
10	Twist center of gross liver (6)	8	Beatle beginners jump over harmony news (4)
11	I am regularly smarmy (3)	9	Joy takes a glimpse of elegant Friends character (4)

Girls Names Cryptic (B&P & Letter Sequence Clues)

In this cryptic crossword, all answers are popular girls' names. Also, all clues use bits and pieces clues or letter sequence clues. The sections of the clue are not highlighted for you. Good luck!

Hints on pg 53, Answers on pg 64

	ACROSS		DOWN
1	Princess heads down interesting avenue near Amsterdam (5)	1	Doll with head of yak sings Jolene (5)
2	Well, Ben heads off to talk show host (5)	3	Book of the Bible comes from drop of scotch in ether (6)
6	Steal mummy, even for Melissa McCarthy movie (5)	4	Winehouse is a heartless meany (3)
9	Finally, crush tea down in aroma cloth for Montana (6)	5	Ms. Bullock found sand on the borders of Russia (6)
11	Adam's wife is in the middle of fever (3)	7	Former first lady has initially lovely aura (5)
12	Carl eats bit of omelet with Burnett (5)	8	Firstly, lady, i love you and Tomlin (4)
13	Can Uncle Andrew have seconds, Kendrick? (4)	10	Rudolph evens out meaty man (4)

Instrument Cryptic (B&P & Letter Sequence Review - Highlighted)

In this cryptic crossword, all answers are instruments. The sections of the clue are highlighted for you. The straight part is in blue, hidden word indicators are in green, reversal indicators are in dark green, anagram indicators are in orange, homophone word indicators are in purple, additions are light yellow, deletions are dark yellow, abbreviations are pink, bits and pieces indicators are red, and letter sequence indicators are in teal. Good luck!

Answers on pg 65

	ACROSS		DOWN
1	Imp captured by tan one sits in the back of the orchestra (7)	1	Lastly, can't you scrub a large brass instrument? (4)
4	Graduate with New Jersey, Oscar plays in a bluegrass band (5)	2	Fibber talks about stringed instrument (4)
5	Part of charm on Icarus turns breath into music (9)	3	Theo books secret retreat for double-reed (4)
8	Rocky earns drum (5)	6	Small accordion is wrongly into cancer (10)
11	Star has last Israeli instrument (5)	7	Spooner plays B chord on long instrument (8)
12	Integral variation for shape (8)	9	Plucked instrument is even flauntier (4)
13	Topless Morgan plays at church (5)	10	Orchestra member from cell close to Toronto (5)

Alcohol Cryptic (B&P & Letter Sequence Review)

In this cryptic crossword, all answers are types of alcohol. The sections of the clue are not highlighted for you. Good luck!

Hints on pg 53, Answers on pg 65

	ACROSS		DOWN
2	Banish E.T. roughly for alcohol (8)	1	Alcohol for Pam, Shane, and Spooner (9)
5	Al took bite of egg for alcohol (3)	2	A mare joins tenor to make alcohol (8)
6	Oddly slap knee for Japanese alcohol (4)	3	She leads rowdy raccoon yoga for alcohol (6)
7	Other umbrella conceals alcohol (3)	4	Reportedly key on tea makes alcohol (7)
9	Be our bishop on alcohol (7)	8	Alcohol from crazy dame (4)
12	Headless swine make people drunk (4)	9	Brando nearly joined club for alcohol (6)
13	Alcohol appears in freak dove somersault (5)	10	Alcohol made from bee and bear tail (4)
14	Alcohol spoiled key wish (7)	11	Alcohol is central to aging (3)

Rarer Wordplay Clues

These next clues are a bit rarer than the ones we've already discussed. Some of these clues only work on very specific words, so they do not show up as often as others. So we will introduce 5 types of them to you now to practice.

Letter Bank Clues

Letter Bank clues are a newer addition to the wordplay options since cryptic crosswords began. These clues indicate that all the unique letters of the (typically long) answer can be found in a smaller word or words. (This smaller part should only use each unique letter once, creating an isogram)

For example, the word LENS is a word bank for the longer word SENSELESSNESS.

LETTER BANK INDICATORS

Using every element as needed	Ingredients	Has all the components	Provides everything you need

The straight clues are in blue. The letter bank indicators are in brown.

Cryptic Clue	Answer	Explanation
Pic den holds all the ingredients for freedom (12)	INDEPENDENCE	The letters PICDEN hold all the unique letters for INDEPENDENCE
Gamin provides everything for Italian actress (4,7)	ANNA MAGNANI	The letters GAMIN hold all the unique letters for ANNA MAGNANI

Cryptic Clues

Cryptic definitions are popular amongst constructors. You're not given wordplay per se, rather the word is defined in a way that requires lateral thinking. They are basically single or double definitions, and one of the definitions is a creative, clever way of thinking. These clues are often indicated by using a question mark.

Examples:

Cryptic Clue	Answer	Explanation
Elaborate gesture like something made of wheat? (8)	FLOURISH	Wheat could mean the word 'flour', so something made of wheat might be flour-ish.
Die of cold? (3,4)	ICE CUBE	Here, die refers to a single dice, or a cube. And a cube that is cold would be an ice cube!

Double Definition Clues

Double definition clues have no indicator words! These clues have two definitions right next to each other. These words are all homographs, which means they are spelled the same, but have different meanings, and possibly different pronunciations.

Both straight clues are in blue.

Cryptic Clue	Answer	Explanation
Break open chest (4)	BUST	Bust, as a verb, means to break open something, and bust, as a noun, refers to a woman's chest
Small unit of time (6)	MINUTE	Minute, pronounced 'minit', is a unit of time, while minute, pronounced 'my newt', means small

Charades Clues

Charades clues take their name from the popular game of Charades, where one player acts out the answer by splitting the word into digestible sections.

The straight clue is in blue. The charades wordplay clue is underlined.

Cryptic Clue	Answer	Explanation
Rock group gets older while dressing (8)	BANDAGES	A rock group is a 'band'. Gets older means 'ages', and 'bandages' is a dressing for wounds.
Carport for average ruler (7)	PARKING	Average means 'par'. Ruler could mean 'king'. PAR + KING = PARKING

&Lit Clues

&Lit clues stand for '& Literally So'. These are wildly creative clues that act as both the definition AND the wordplay. You can identify these clues by an exclamation mark! These types of clues are quite rare, so if you find one, enjoy!

The straight part (the entire clue) will be underlined.
Other wordplay indicators will be their regular highlighted color.

Cryptic Clue	Answer	Explanation
I'm a Muslim leader! (4)	IMAM	'Muslim leader' gives the letter M. Add the 'I'm a" to get IMAM, which is a Muslim leader!
Hearing part! (3)	EAR	Part means a hidden section of the word 'hearing'. And an ear is a hearing part!

Bird Cryptic (Rarer Wordplay Clues - Highlighted)

In this cryptic crossword, all answers are birds. The sections of the clue are highlighted for you. The straight part(s) are in blue, the letter bank indicators are in brown, the (?)s mean cryptic clues, and the (!)s and underline mean &Lit clues. Anything not highlighted is likely charades. Good luck!

Answers on pg 66

	ACROSS		DOWN
2	Consume bird (7)	1	Nectar lover that purrs? (11)
4	Dodge bird (4)	2	Baby bird? (5)
8	Sea bird uses every element of flute body as needed (4-6,5)	3	Nightly singer to lash unfortunate bequest (12)
10	Initially inspiring bird in stream! (4)	5	Bird plummeted (4)
11	Fight twice for songbird (7)	6	Semi-backbone in a pear tree? (9)
13	Rondeau provides everything for Coyote's prey (10)	7	Lost bra has everything you need - that's a bad sign (9)
15	Prowler at heart! (3)	9	Bird is swine age (6)
16	Cowardly poultry (7)	12	Average decay forms talking bird (6)
17	Bird voices Genie in Aladdin (5)	14	Bird fence (4)

Plant Cryptic (Rarer Wordplay Clues)

In this cryptic crossword, all answers are plants. Also, all clues use either letter banks, charades, double definitions, &lit, or cryptic wordplay. The sections of the clue are not highlighted for you. Good luck!

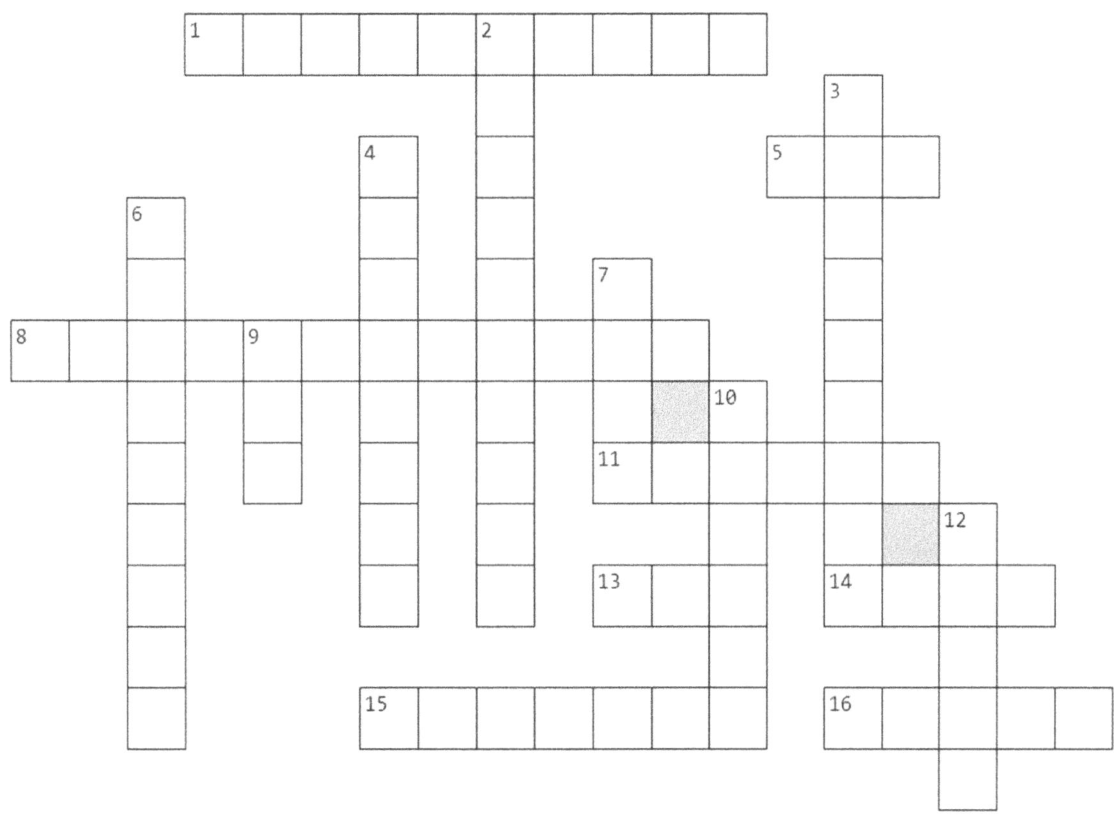

Hints on pg 54, Answers on pg 66

	ACROSS		DOWN
1	Evening blinds? (10)	2	Old swan gives everything to yellow tree (10)
5	Regret shrub (3)	3	Container of fat? (9)
8	No, my girl has everything needed for September flower (7,5)	4	Handwear for vixen? (8)
11	Tidy up tree (6)	6	Flower in vehicle country (9)
13	Tree created by burnt wood (3)	7	Flower found in eye (4)
14	Tree in center of hand (4)	9	Starting to inch along sides of vinery! (3)
15	Follow golf club to flaky tree (7)	10	Brutish monster stashes flower (6)
16	What hens eat when leaving Athens! (5)	12	Tree is not younger (5)

Herbs & Spices Cryptic (Rarer Wordplay Review - Highlighted)

In this cryptic crossword, all answers are herbs and spices. The sections of the clue are highlighted for you. The straight part is in blue, the hidden word indicators are in green, reversal indicators are in dark green, anagram indicators are in orange, homophone word indicators are in purple, additions are light yellow, deletions are dark yellow, abbreviations are pink, bits and pieces indicators are red, letter sequence indicators are in teal, letter bank indicators are in brown, (?)s mean cryptic clues, and the (!)s and underline mean &Lit clues. Anything not highlighted is likely charades. Good luck!

Answers on pg 67

	ACROSS		DOWN
3	Check the ID of a parent? (8)	1	Expensive spice for fans by mistake (7)
7	Gutted uplander interrupted cry for spice (5)	2	Wise herb (4)
8	Vinegar licorice disguises what Dracula hates (6)	4	Even coarser grains of herb (7)
10	Print me all the ingredients for an aromatic (10)	5	Charlie has love for pumpkin spice (5)
11	Pinches of aromatics needed in seasoning everything! (5)	6	Spice reportedly found in tumor. Ick (8)
13	Messy tan rag or savory herb (8)	9	Two ladies work together for Herb (8)
14	Lisa B. came back for Herb (5)	12	Herb master leaves treadmills (4)

Collective Animal Names Cryptic (Rarer Wordplay Review)

In this cryptic crossword, all answers are collective animal names. The sections of the clue are not highlighted for you. Good luck!

Hints are on pg 54, Answers on pg 67

	ACROSS		DOWN
6	Loan curd around to group of bats (8)	1	Shot scattered group of sparrows (4)
7	Group of vipers invest, then lose $4 (4)	2	Kill group of crows (6)
10	Criminal occupation for group of eagles (11)	3	Group of porcupines adds drop of ranch inside pickle (7)
11	Group of elephants spar a demon fragment (6)	4	Group of ravens find all they need in used ink (10)
12	Pack of dolphins initially! (3)	5	Nothing found in flat group of crocodiles (5)
13	Heard broadcast for group of antelope (4)	8	Group of giraffes is a hauler of broken vehicles? (5)
15	Group of stingrays run a temperature (5)	9	Taller rabbit holds back group of monkeys (6)
16	Group of owls agitated mental pair (10)	14	Group of oysters found in bread; odd (3)

Combination Clues

Combination clues are just what they sound like. These types of clues combine multiple wordplay types to make extra-creative cryptic clues.

The straight definition is in blue. The wordplay section is underlined. Hidden word indicators are in green. Reversal indicators are in dark green. Anagram indicators are in orange. Homophone indicators are in purple. Additions/Deletions indicators are in yellow. Abbreviations are in pink. Bits & Pieces indicators are in red. Letter Sequence indicators are in teal.

Cryptic Clue	Answer	Explanation
Flower girl hid ring in really small enclosure, initially (4)	ROSE	Ring can be abbreviated O, because it looks like a ring. The letter sequence clue tells us to look at the initials of 'really small enclosure', so RSE. O inside RSE makes ROSE.
Silly Olivia spent $5 on sauce (5)	AIOLI	Anagram Olivia, but subtract V (5 in Roman Numerals). OLIIA = AIOLI
Micki's partner is mad about you, egghead! (5)	MAUDE	'You' stands for U. Mad is around (about) U. Egghead means head of egg, which is E. MAUD + E = MAUDE

Indirect Clues

As part of this beginner's guide, I've intentionally left most of the clues very straight forward. There wasn't much that you needed to define, because the wordplay was obvious. However, many regular cryptic crosswords will make the wordplay *indirect*. Similar to the homophone clues, you'll need to think about what words match the definitions before some wordplay is done.

<u>Note</u>: You'll never need to anagram a word if it's not included in the question directly!

The straight definition is in blue. The wordplay section is underlined. The indirect words are in *italics*

Cryptic Clue	Answer	Explanation
Pastry right on dock (4)	PIER	Pastry means PIE. Right is abbreviated R. PIE + R = PIER
Greenhouse took out *fish* to study (3)	DEN	Greenhouse could mean GARDEN. Fish, then, means GAR. GARDEN - GAR = DEN
Report Ann with *measurement* (8)	ANNOUNCE	Measurement could be many things, but here it means OUNCE. ANN + OUNCE = ANNOUNCE
Believe in true *oxidation* (5)	TRUST	True is abbreviated T. Oxidation means RUST. T + RUST = TRUST

5-Letter Cryptic 1 (Everything Review - Highlighted)

In this cryptic crossword, all answers are 5-letter words. The sections of the clue are highlighted for you. The straight part is in blue, the hidden word indicators are in green, reversal indicators are in dark green, anagram indicators are in orange, homophone word indicators are in purple, additions are light yellow, deletions are dark yellow, abbreviations are pink, bits and pieces indicators are red, letter sequence indicators are in teal, letter bank indicators are in brown, ?s mean cryptic clues, and the !s and underline mean &Lit clues. Anything not highlighted is likely charades. *Italics* indicate an indirect word clue. Good luck!

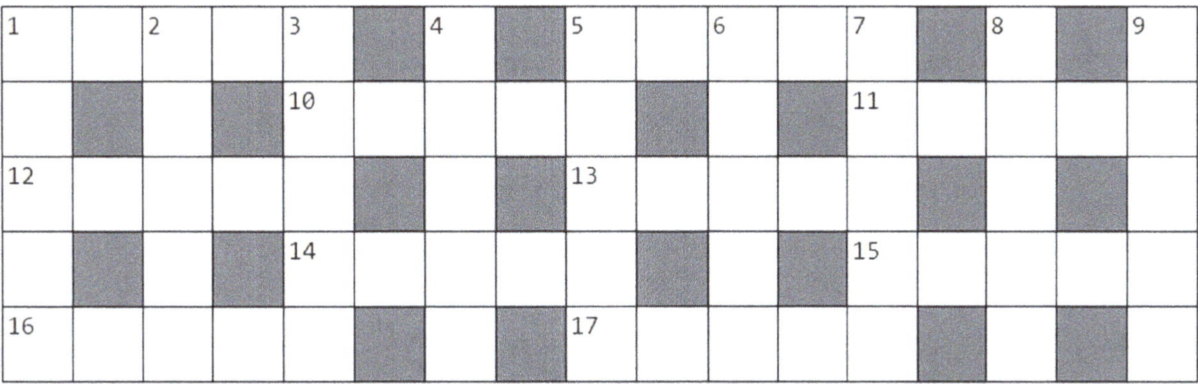

Answers on pg 68

	ACROSS		DOWN
1	Repel lunatic! (5)	1	Actual run? (5)
5	Frighten *healed wound* with energy (5)	2	Ran within park borders as a joke (5)
10	Illuminated silver *bass* (5)	3	Conrad only contains an element (5)
11	*Stupid person* almost joined Mike with expression (5)	4	Oddly follow Nazis to remove food (5)
12	A bit of gray *ground* is where sweat comes from (5)	5	Southwest one with possum heart from Bern, perhaps? (5)
13	I sing on the radio and top cakes (5)	6	A note with half-goat friend (5)
14	Love a *bro's sibling* in paradise (5)	7	Alien consumed one German husband and octet (5)
15	Central hotel has crazy rate (5)	8	See, I *fish* for a tobacco product (5)
16	*Hobbit author* rejected large island for symbol (5)	9	Vacate my pet wrongly (5)
17	Missing brief (5)		

5-Letter Cryptic 2 (Everything Review)

In this cryptic crossword, all answers are 5-letter words. The sections of the clue are not highlighted for you. *Italics* will still help you with indirect word clues. Good luck!

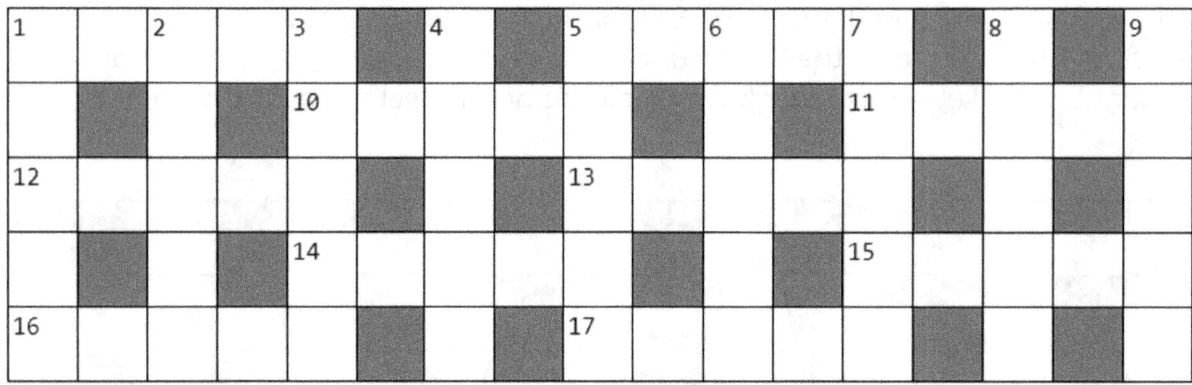

Hints are on pg 55, Answers on pg 69

	ACROSS		DOWN
1	Pumpkin pierced with sharp object audibly (5)	1	Hideous green category (5)
5	Sweep right inside *loud noise* (5)	2	Knock over trouble (5)
10	Redhead up and wide awake finally gives Indian money (5)	3	Doctor eats rye to get less wet (5)
11	Pottery removed shell, revealed water weasel (5)	4	Small flame fragment in gross parking (5)
12	No singular European club is inquisitive (5)	5	*Grizzly* gains 500 chin hairs (5)
13	The Little Mermaid is real, meandering around island (5)	6	Yes, French and German used to communicate with the dead (5)
14	Problem with *fish eggs* falling back over railroad (5)	7	Month old whiskey finally is rotten (5)
15	Oddly, doesn't even Usher become ignorant? (5)	8	Knits wrong way from unpleasant smell (5)
16	Invade center; lose head (5)	9	Distressed Lucifer excluded if grim (5)
17	*Help* returned to heartless Rodney with journal (5)		

How to Solve a Typical Cryptic Crossword

You've learned tons of wordplay and tested your knowledge on over 20 different puzzles, but cracking a NY Times cryptic crossword is still a challenge. Here are some tips for reading these clues and where to start.

1. Read the clue... multiple times. Read it slowly. Try your best to read it as individual words and don't get caught up in the surface reading.
2. Look at the first word(s) and last word(s). This is where the straight definition will be hiding.
   a. Ex. **Power tool made doctor sick (5)**
   b. The definition could be **Power, Power tool, or sick.**
3. Look for indicator words you may be familiar with.
   a. Crazy/weird/messy are often anagram indicators
   b. Anything to do with sound (hearing, say, listen) might mean a homophone
   c. Look for abbreviations! New is often N. Old is often O. States and countries often get abbreviated. Have your list handy!
4. Make note of different options for wordplay.
   a. Ex. **Power tool made doctor sick (5)**
   b. **Power** can be abbreviated to P
   c. **Tool** might be any short tool, like an AWL, AXE or SAW.
   d. **Doctor** can be many abbreviations, including DR, MD, GP and more.
   e. **Sick** could mean ILL.
5. Do NOT be fooled by the surface reading. This clue seems like the answer will be about a hospital tool, but this is the distracting portion that leads you away from the clever wordplay and answer.
6. Look at the enumeration. The number of letters can help you immensely when it comes to what wordplay forms the clue uses.
   a. Ex. **Power tool made doctor sick (5)**
   b. So far, it looks like this word will be made up of smaller words and letters. What options can we choose from to make a 5-letter word?
7. If you have other letters on the board, this will help you! Sometimes you can guess the resulting word just from the letters you have already filled in.
8. Move on to other questions if you have to. Don't waste too much time ruminating over a difficult clue. Look for clues that are short (likely double definitions) and fill in the board as best you can. You don't have to play the clues in order!
9. Ignore any punctuation or capitalization. Only sometimes with a question mark alert you to a cryptic definition.
10. Play cryptic crosswords more! The more you practice, the better you'll be at solving them!

On the next pages, you'll find two 'typical' cryptic crosswords. I'm calling them typical because they use the square-shaped board with at least half of each word's letters checked with other clues. Good luck solving them!

Answer: DRILL

Typical Cryptic 1 (Highlighted)

In this cryptic crossword, there is **no theme**. The sections of the clue are highlighted for you. The straight part is in blue, the hidden word indicators are in green, reversal indicators are in dark green, anagram indicators are in orange, homophone word indicators are in purple, additions are light yellow, deletions are dark yellow, abbreviations are pink, bits and pieces indicators are red, letter sequence indicators are in teal, letter bank indicators are in brown, (?)s mean cryptic clues, and the (!)s and underline mean &Lit clues. Anything not highlighted is likely charades. *Italics* indicate an indirect word clue. Good luck!

Answers on pg 70

	ACROSS				DOWN		
1	Reuse plug awkwardly as adhesive (5,4)	16	Oddly, armhole has degree in single-cell (6)	1	Southern alien is ready (3)	12	A *barrier* for first man (4)
6	*Spanish agree* with Republican mister (3)	19	Momma lost head and fell back from bullets (4)	2	Deception is per judge and old city youth, originally (7)	14	Celebrity mark (4)
8	Spooner has sore toe in trunk (5)	21	Proclaim building cleared (7)	3	Shape *Greek letter* with grand bus (7)	17	Mike and Oscar? No, Cleo mostly makes glass (7)
9	Alabama University headmaster kept back sun for graduate (7)	24	Wild Aslan is sharp (5)	4	Detest a hotel madly (6)	18	Awful end user is guaranteed (7)
10	Husband, male, sits in tub as leaf (5)	25	South African knight and gold soldier all turn back from reptiles (7)	5	Fellow eastern queen leads unusually artistic lifestyle (5)	20	EMS has everything you need and creates disorder (6)
11	50% works about yearly, at first, and partly (7)	26	Reef sings composition made for choir (5)	6	Muscle is sin, you said (5)	22	Throw away Norris (5)
13	Hand-me-down is half confused (4)	28	Remodel kitchen exhibiting deer (3)	7	Scotch cocktail took heads off crusty snail (5,4)	23	A new north duck? Why bother? (5)
15	Quiet! Heartless yeast is most bashful (6)	29	*You archaically* strayed by mistake in the past (9)	10	The heartless saint has *desire* for tryout (4,5)	27	Put down most of *popular chip brand* (3)

Typical Cryptic 2

In this cryptic crossword, there is no theme. The sections of the clue are not highlighted for you. *Italics* still indicate an indirect word clue. Good luck!

Hints on pg 56, Answers on pg 71

	ACROSS				DOWN		
1	*Lay asphalt* westbound, *give a speech* and disappear (9)	16	Indifference in a *route* unknown (6)	1	Retype evenly for scan (3)	12	Bird from southwest came to North America fixed up (4)
6	Illness hovered, they say (3)	19	Single credit announced (4)	2	Al virtually bans Iowa from European country (7)	14	Moving early without a bank (4)
8	Nudge the Spanish *ship* end (5)	21	Burros *wear essentials* (7)	3	Ahead, old and new *hospital rooms* (7)	17	Odd poetry for grand present (7)
9	Some mar hub arbitrarily for celery cousin (7)	24	Branch first cut for plantation (5)	4	Large arteries give ear to a malfunction (6)	18	Oven emptied within tight evening today (7)
10	Door admitted new giver (5)	25	Dream team pick is *completely lead* (3-4)	5	Provide electronic *joke* (5)	20	Windows *not predator* for bird (6)
11	Raisin exploded with drop of paint and medicine (7)	26	Should tough leader move to the end? (5)	6	Fir around city has talent (5)	22	The Reverend says, "Lie non-fibers" (5)
13	Sketched interest (4)	28	A billion years for one problem (3)	7	Burn my hat by mistake in folklore story (5,4)	23	Additional former lover returned art (5)
15	*Listen* closer to ominous echo from funeral car (6)	29	A mystery strangely contained scrap of mold from lopsidedness (9)	10	Heat Ed dry in a whirl! (9)	27	Attempt to time river variable (3)

Remember Your First Cryptic Crossword?

Here is the same cryptic crossword you saw at the beginning of this manual! Hopefully it looks a bit less daunting now that you've learned about the different kinds of wordplay. Have a go at solving it now!

Hints on pg 56, Answers on pg 72

	ACROSS				DOWN		
1	Power source found in faux eel, oddly (4)	13	Fruit with tulip core is a valuable item (5)	1	Bewilder mist (3)	11	Circle part of Bob or Derek (6)
3	Sorority leader tags male deer (5)	16	Period of time sounds like yours and mine (3)	2	Attorney returned real Wyoming stuffing (6)	12	Half of plainest home (4)
6	Glare from exhausted general with a cry of pain (4)	17	Go inside any affliction (5)	3	Small lime ooze (5)	13	Illegally hunt quiet Oscar at empty athletic hospital (5)
8	Popular key with English coordinate! (5)	18	Ta-da, corrected information (4)	4	Hearing gold God from Italy (5)	14	Float around in the air (5)
9	Tuber month making a come back (3)	20	Furious with the Spanish inn (5)	5	Three score and nine Romans stuck in pigpen (5)	15	Play old segment back true (5)
10	Box of nuts originally filled every case of dark wood (5)	21	Bridge monster dropped tea to spin (4)	7	Path created by Louisiana and Nebraska (4)	19	Entire mall won't start (3)

HINTS

All of these hints highlight the wordplay for the clues. The straight definition is in blue. Hidden word indicators are in green. Reversal indicators are in dark green. Anagram indicators are in orange. Homophone indicators are in purple. Additions/Deletions indicators are in yellow. Abbreviations are in pink. Bits & Pieces indicators are in red. Letter Sequence indicators are in teal. Letter Bank indicators are in brown. (?)s mean Cryptic clues. (!)s and underline mean <u>&Lit clues</u>. Anything not highlighted is likely Charades. *Italics* indicate an Indirect word clue.

US Presidents on pg 11

Answers on pg 57

	ACROSS		DOWN
3	Seventh president partly hijacks onlookers (7)	1	No sir, Rahab attributes overturning to ninth president (8)
5	First president conceals brainwashing tongue (10)	2	Mice or no mice? Some back the fifth president (6)
8	38th president is partly affordable (4)	4	Nomad is on displays as fourth president (7)
9	27th president is buried in hot fat rearwards (4)	6	Peg ran towards content of 18th president (5)
11	20th president dwells in sugar fields (8)	7	Some psycho overreacts to 31st president (6)
12	Component of plush Subaru recalled for 43rd president (4)	10	Plasma dances upright secretly for the second president (5)

Mythical Creatures on pg 14

Answers on pg 58

	ACROSS		DOWN
6	A peer lunch may be found on St. Patrick's Day (10)	1	Correctly uncrate half man half horse (7)
9	Flaming bird mishandles oxen hip (7)	2	Drunkenly nag Rod for giant reptile (6)
10	Cook me a rich Greek monster (7)	3	I revamp strange blood-sucker (7)
12	Gore turned into a green monster (4)	4	Fantastic horse may incur no corruption (7)
13	I fry a naughty pixie (5)	5	Gene, I could be one who grants wishes (5)
14	I tye badly for an abominable snowman (4)	8	Disguise gem on garden creature (5)
15	Sh, got wild spirit? (5)	8	Flying horse has Pa guess loosely (7)
16	Awful tumor in a bullish man (8)	11	Mischievous creature rambles in blog (6)

Fruit on pg 16

Answers on pg 59

	ACROSS		DOWN
3	Fruit has curious lump (4)	1	Fruit found in panda tent (4)
6	Giftwrap ricotta inside fruit (7)	2	Nope. Actual trouble is fruit (10)
8	Fruit interfered with mile (4)	3	Hippo, Meg, ran at Evelyn hiding fruit (11)
10	Reap unusual fruit (4)	4	Letters from Cuban; a natural fruit (6)
11	An ogre jumbled fruit (6)	5	Khaki wizard disguises fruit (4)
12	Piece of fungiform reversed fruit (3)	7	Fruit ruined pagers (6)
13	Wildly cheap fruit (5)	9	Fruit demonstrates human goals (5)

Types of People on pg 19

Answers on pg 60

	ACROSS		DOWN
1	Spooner asks, "Say, men lay bricks?" (5)	2	Nothing on the radio, sister (3)
3	Uncle's wife sounds like tiny insect (4)	4	Private teacher is a person who plays the horn audibly (5)
6	Nobleman overheard evening darkness (6)	5	"Hem clothes later." says the Reverend (6)
9	Ranked official is related to war, by the sound of it (7)	7	Drug mumbled to female hero (7)
11	Poet is not allowed to enter hearing (4)	8	"Make money!", announced oracle (7)
14	School head told fundamental truth (9)	10	Person in sales reported basement (6)
15	Candy packaging in audition as spoken word musician (6)	12	Asking for specifying information outloud for enchantress (5)
16	I heard broiler is a religious monk (5)	13	Broadcast decorative knot for lover boy (4)

Countries on pg 21

Answers on pg 61

	ACROSS		DOWN
1	Partially kidnap a jaguar. Bring back to Asian island country (5)	1	Acai jam ordered from Caribbean country (7)
3	Dairy store dwells back in Middle Eastern country (5)	2	South American country is kind of pure (4)
4	Funny aroma in European country (7)	6	Rebel, I zest secretly for Caribbean country (6)
5	Glitch in atoms conceal rich country (5)	8	Type 'G' randomly for pharaoh's home (5)
7	Balkan country reported oily substance (6)	9	Mediterranean island listens to evergreen tree (6)
10	Nairobi's country hidden in broken yacht (5)	10	Spooner says,"Woo Kate in the Middle East" (6)
12	Aga, our quiet alien, transformed west African country (10,6)	11	Ringwald heard landlocked African country (4)

<u>Hints continued</u>

Round Things on pg 27

Answers on pg 62

	ACROSS		DOWN
4	One small boy in free flying saucer (7)	1	Tango or till a burrito staple (8)
6	See lock tell time (5)	2	Remove senior from shrub, find center of wheel (3)
7	South Africa has two notes about sandwich meat (6)	3	Gourd from Maine left nothing new (5)
8	Bag the Spanish breakfast roll (5)	5	Loud instrument is going without iodine (4)
10	Pressure Earl to form within an oyster (5)	9	Fruit of oak tree is alpha corn (5)
12	Four within ole martini garnish (5)	10	Pen by New York is one cent (5)
13	Moron ignored right, like Io or Titan (4)	11	Brings guillotine for marriage symbols (5)

Bugs on pg 29

Answers on pg 63

	ACROSS		DOWN
2	Tiny insect pant initially rejected (3)	1	Month, not November, loves the light (4)
5	Messy rags he props for flighty bug (11)	3	Fly can't set sermon secretly (6)
6	Graph identified hidden plantsucker (5)	4	Belgium alien left Earth for pest (6)
7	Flighty bug clouts roughly (6)	5	Tiny insect sends up tang (4)
10	Audibly run away from small insect (4)	8	CIA imprisons California democrat who makes loud buzzing noises (6)
11	Crazy spy marinating with holy bug? (7,6)	9	Sail captures new slimy mollusk (5)
13	I see inside the French head bugs (4)	12	Bloodsucking creature has habitual movement, reportedly (4)

Girls Names on pg 33

Answers on pg 64

ACROSS		DOWN	
1	Princess heads down interesting avenue near Amsterdam (5)	1	Doll with head of yak sings Jolene (5)
2	Well, Ben heads off to talk show host (5)	3	Book of the Bible comes from drop of scotch in ether (6)
6	Steal mummy, even for Melissa McCarthy movie (5)	4	Winehouse is a heartless meany (3)
9	Finally, crush tea down in aroma cloth for Montana (6)	5	Ms. Bullock found sand on the borders of Russia (6)
11	Adam's wife is in the middle of fever (3)	7	Former first lady has initially lovely aura (5)
12	Carl eats bit of omelet with Burnett (5)	8	Firstly, lady, i love you and Tomlin (4)
13	Can Uncle Andrew have seconds, Kendrick? (4)	10	Rudolph evens out meaty man (4)

Alcohol on pg 35

Answers on pg 65

ACROSS		DOWN	
2	Banish E.T. roughly for alcohol (8)	1	Alcohol for Pam, Shane, and Spooner (9)
5	Al took bite of egg for alcohol (3)	2	A mare joins tenor to make alcohol (8)
6	Oddly slap knee for Japanese alcohol (4)	3	She leads rowdy raccoon yoga for alcohol (6)
7	Other umbrella conceals alcohol (3)	4	Reportedly key on tea makes alcohol (7)
9	Be our bishop on alcohol (7)	8	Alcohol from crazy dame (4)
12	Headless swine make people drunk (4)	9	Brando nearly joined club for alcohol (6)
13	Alcohol appears in freak dove somersault (5)	10	Alcohol made from bee and bear tail (4)
14	Alcohol spoiled key wish (7)	11	Alcohol is central to aging (3)

Plants on pg 39

Answers on pg 66

	ACROSS		DOWN
1	Evening blinds? (10)	2	Old swan gives everything to yellow tree (10)
5	Regret shrub (3)	3	Container of fat? (9)
8	No, my girl has everything needed for September flower (7,5)	4	Handwear for vixen? (8)
11	Tidy up tree (6)	6	Flower in vehicle country (9)
13	Tree created by burnt wood (3)	7	Flower found in eye (4)
14	Tree in center of hand (4)	9	Starting to inch along sides of vinery! (3)
15	Follow golf club to flaky tree (7)	10	Brutish monster stashes flower (6)
16	What hens eat when leaving Athens! (5)	12	Tree is not younger (5)

Collective Animal Names on pg 41

Answers on pg 67

	ACROSS		DOWN
6	Loan curd around to group of bats (8)	1	Shot scattered group of sparrows (4)
7	Group of vipers invest, then lose $4 (4)	2	Kill group of crows (6)
10	Criminal occupation for group of eagles (11)	3	Group of porcupines adds drop of ranch inside pickle (7)
11	Group of elephants spar a demon fragment (6)	4	Group of ravens find all they need in used ink (10)
12	Pack of dolphins initially! (3)	5	Nothing found in flat group of crocodiles (5)
13	Heard broadcast for group of antelope (4)	8	Group of giraffes is a hauler of broken vehicles? (5)
15	Group of stingrays run a temperature (5)	9	Taller rabbit holds back group of monkeys (6)
16	Group of owls agitated mental pair (10)	14	Group of oysters found in bread; odd (3)

5-Letter Words on pg 44

Answers on pg 69

	ACROSS		DOWN
1	Pumpkin pierced with sharp object audibly (5)	1	Hideous green category (5)
5	Sweep right inside *loud noise* (5)	2	Knock over trouble (5)
10	Redhead up and wide awake finally gives Indian money (5)	3	Doctor eats rye to get less wet (5)
11	Pottery removed shell, revealed water weasel (5)	4	Small flame fragment in gross parking (5)
12	No singular European club is inquisitive (5)	5	*Grizzly* gains 500 chin hairs (5)
13	The Little Mermaid is real, meandering around island (5)	6	Yes, French and German used to communicate with the dead (5)
14	Problem with *fish eggs* falling back over railroad (5)	7	Month old whiskey finally is rotten (5)
15	Oddly, doesn't even Usher become ignorant? (5)	8	Knits wrong way from unpleasant smell (5)
16	Invade center; lose head (5)	9	Distressed Lucifer excluded if grim (5)
17	*Help* returned to heartless Rodney with journal (5)		

<u>**Hints continued**</u>

Typical Cryptic 2 on pg 47

Answers on pg 71

	ACROSS				DOWN		
1	*Lay asphalt* westbound, *give a speech* and disappear (9)	16	Indifference in a *route* unknown (6)	1	Retype evenly for scan (3)	12	Bird from southwest came to North America fixed up (4)
6	Illness hovered, they say (3)	19	Single credit announced (4)	2	A1 virtually bans Iowa from European country (7)	14	Moving early without a bank (4)
8	Nudge the Spanish *ship end* (5)	21	Burros *wear essentials* (7)	3	Ahead, old and new *hospital rooms* (7)	17	Odd poetry for grand present (7)
9	Some mar hub arbitrarily for celery cousin (7)	24	Branch first cut for plantation (5)	4	Large arteries give ear to a malfunction (6)	18	Oven emptied within tight evening today (7)
10	Door admitted new giver (5)	25	Dream team pick is *completely lead* (3-4)	5	Provide electronic *joke* (5)	20	Windows *not predator* for bird (6)
11	Raisin exploded with drop of paint and medicine (7)	26	Should tough leader move to the end? (5)	6	Fir around city has talent (5)	22	The Reverend says, "Lie non-fibers" (5)
13	Sketched interest (4)	28	A billion years for one problem (3)	7	Burn my hat by mistake in folklore story (5,4)	23	Additional former lover returned art (5)
15	*Listen* closer to ominous echo from funeral car (6)	29	A mystery strangely contained scrap of mold from lopsidedness (9)	10	<u>Heat Ed dry in a whirl!</u> (9)	27	Attempt to time river variable (3)

Your First Cryptic on pg 6 & 48

Answers on pg 72

	ACROSS				DOWN		
1	Power source found in faux eel, oddly (4)	13	*Fruit with tulip* core is a valuable item (5)	1	Bewilder mist (3)	11	Circle part of Bob or Derek (6)
3	Sorority leader tags male deer (5)	16	*Period of time* sounds like yours and mine (3)	2	Attorney returned real Wyoming stuffing (6)	12	Half of plainest home (4)
6	Glare from exhausted general with *a cry of pain* (4)	17	Go inside any affliction (5)	3	Small lime ooze (5)	13	Illegally hunt quiet Oscar at empty athletic hospital (5)
8	<u>Popular key with English coordinate!</u> (5)	18	Ta-da, corrected information (4)	4	Hearing gold *God from Italy* (5)	14	Float around in the air (5)
9	Tuber *month* making a come back (3)	20	*Furious* with the Spanish inn (5)	5	Three score and nine Romans stuck in *pigpen* (5)	15	Play old segment back true (5)
10	Box of nuts originally filled every case of dark wood (5)	21	*Bridge monster* dropped tea to spin (4)	7	Path created by Louisiana and Nebraska (4)	19	Entire mall won't start (3)

ANSWERS

HIDDEN WORDS ONLY

Christmas Words on pg 10

ACROSS			DOWN		
#	Answer	Explanation	#	Answer	Explanation
3	GREEN	Green is hidden backwards: engi_neer grows_	1	CIDER	Cider is hidden: Ran_cid era_ser
5	HYMN	Hymn is hidden backwards: sin_; my h_ope	2	SANTA CLAUS	Santa Claus is hidden backwards: Unu_sual cat nas_tiness
7	TINSEL	Tinsel is hidden: brough_t in sel_ect	4	RUDOLPH	Rudolph is hidden backwards: fis_h plod ur_gently
9	GARLAND	Garland is hidden: Cou_gar lande_d	6	SNOW	Snow is hidden: There'_s no way_
10	ELF	Elf is hidden: w_elf_are	8	EGGNOG	Eggnog is hidden backwards: Du_gong ge_ts
11	WORSHIP	Worship is hidden: cre_w or ship_mate	12	STAR	Star is hidden: mu_star_dy

US Presidents on pg 11

ACROSS			DOWN		
#	Answer	Explanation	#	Answer	Explanation
3	JACKSON	Jackson is hidden: hi_jacks on_lookers	1	HARRISON	Harrison is hidden backwards: No _sir, Raha_b
5	WASHINGTON	Washington is hidden: brain_washing ton_gue	2	MONROE	Monroe is hidden backwards: Mic_e or no m_ice
8	FORD	Ford is hidden: af_ford_able	4	MADISON	Madison is hidden: No_mad is on_
9	TAFT	Taft is hidden backwards: ho_t fat_	6	GRANT	Grant is hidden: Pe_g ran t_owards
11	GARFIELD	Garfield is hidden: su_gar field_	7	HOOVER	Hoover is hidden: psyc_ho over_reacts
12	BUSH	Bush is hidden backwards: plus_h Su_baru	10	ADAMS	Adams is hidden backwards: Pla_sma da_nces

ANAGRAM WORDS ONLY

Clothing on pg 13

#	Answer	Explanation	#	Answer	Explanation
ACROSS			DOWN		
2	RAINCOAT	Raincoat is an anagram of: Orca ain't	1	MITTENS	Mittens is an anagram of: smitten
4	BLOUSE	Blouse is an anagram of: so blue	3	ASCOT	Ascot is an anagram of: tacos
6	COAT	Coat is an anagram of: A cot	4	BATHROBE	Bathrobe is an anagram of: both bare
7	SWEATER	Sweater is an anagram of: are west	5	SHOES	Shoes is an anagram of: Hoses
10	BRA	Bra is an anagram of: bar	6	CARDIGAN	Cardigan is an anagram of: arcading
11	PAJAMAS	Pajamas is an anagram of: jam a spa	8	GLASSES	Glasses is an anagram of: sag less
12	BOXERS	Boxers is an anagram of: rob sex	9	JEANS	Jeans is an anagram of: as Jen

Mythical Creatures on pg 14

#	Answer	Explanation	#	Answer	Explanation
ACROSS			DOWN		
6	LEPRECHAUN	Leprechaun is an anagram of: A peer lunch	1	CENTAUR	Centaur is an anagram of: uncrate
9	PHOENIX	Phoenix is an anagram of: oxen hip	2	DRAGON	Dragon is an anagram of: nag Rod
10	CHIMERA	Chimera is an anagram of: me a rich	3	VAMPIRE	Vampire is an anagram of: I revamp
12	OGRE	Ogre is an anagram of: Gore	4	UNICORN	Unicorn is an anagram of: incur no
13	FAIRY	Fairy is an anagram of: I fry a	5	GENIE	Genie is an anagram of: Gene, I
14	YETI	Yeti is an anagram of: I tye	7	GNOME	Gnome is an anagram of: gem on
15	GHOST	Ghost is an anagram of: Sh, got	8	PEGASUS	Pegasus is an anagram of: Pa guess
16	MINOTAUR	Minotaur is an anagram of: tumor in a	11	GOBLIN	Goblin is an anagram of: in blog

<u>ANAGRAM REVIEW ONLY</u>

Weather on pg 15

ACROSS			DOWN		
#	Answer	Explanation	#	Answer	Explanation
4	STORM	Storm is an anagram of: Mort's	1	TRACE	Trace is an anagram of: crate
8	AURORA	Aurora is hidden: cent<u>aur or al</u>paca	2	ATMOSPHERE	Atmosphere is an anagram of: ape's mother
9	RAINBOW	Rainbow is hidden: Ok<u>ra in bow</u>l	3	HEATWAVE	Heatwave is an anagram of: Eve, what a
10	EYE	Eye is hidden: g<u>rey e</u>arth	5	MIST	Mist is an anagram of: Ms., it
12	SNOW	Snow is hidden backwards: Bo<u>w ons</u>tage	6	MOISTURE	Moisture is an anagram of: misroute
13	WINDY	Windy is hidden: sorro<u>w in dy</u>stopian	7	OVERCAST	Overcast is hidden: Rec<u>over cast</u>le
14	TEMPERATURE	Temperature is an anagram of: Mature Peter	11	TORNADO	Tornado is an anagram of: donator
15	THUNDER	Thunder is hidden: smoo<u>th underw</u>ear	12	SKY	Sky is hidden: Ri<u>sk y</u>our

Fruit on pg 16

ACROSS			DOWN		
#	Answer	Explanation	#	Answer	Explanation
3	PLUM	Plum is an anagram of: lump	1	DATE	Date is hidden: pan<u>da tent</u>
6	APRICOT	Apricot is hidden: Giftwr<u>ap ricot</u>ta	2	CANTALOUPE	Cantaloupe is an anagram of: Nope. Actual
8	LIME	Lime is an anagram of: mile	3	POMEGRANATE	Pomegranate is hidden: Hip<u>po. Meg. ran at E</u>velyn
10	PEAR	Pear is an anagram of: Reap	4	BANANA	Banana is hidden: Cu<u>ban: a na</u>tural
11	ORANGE	Orange is an anagram of: An ogre	5	KIWI	Kiwi is hidden: Kha<u>ki wi</u>zard
12	FIG	Fig is hidden backward: fun<u>gif</u>orm	7	GRAPES	Grapes is an anagram of: pagers
13	PEACH	Peach is an anagram of: cheap	9	MANGO	Mango is hidden: hu<u>man go</u>als

HOMOPHONE WORDS ONLY

Food on pg 18

	ACROSS			DOWN	
#	Answer	Explanation	#	Answer	Explanation
4	BERRY	Berry sounds like Bury (entomb)	1	PIE	Pie sounds like Pi (Circle constant)
5	MEATBALL	Beat mall is a Spoonerism of Meatball	2	THYME	Thyme sounds like Time (measured by clocks)
6	MOUSSE	Mousse sounds like Moose (large deer)	3	SORBET	Boar,say is a Spoonerism of Sorbet
8	BEET	Beet sounds like Beat (Defeated)	4	BOOZE	Booze sounds like Boos (Ghost noises)
11	LIQUOR	Liquor sounds like Licker (Taster)	7	CHILI	Chili sounds like Chilly (wintry)
12	CARROT	Carrot sounds like Carat (Diamond measurement)	8	BREAD	Bread sounds like Bred (reproduced)
13	WINE	Wine sounds like Whine (complain)	9	TEA	Tea sounds like Tee (Golf assistant)
14	CEREAL	Cereal sounds like Serial (Repeated offender)	10	KERNEL	Kernel sounds like Colonel (Officer)

Types of People on pg 19

	ACROSS			DOWN	
#	Answer	Explanation	#	Answer	Explanation
1	MASON	Say, men is a Spoonerism of Mason	2	NUN	Nun sounds like None (Nothing)
3	AUNT	Aunt sounds like Ant (tiny insect)	4	TUTOR	Tutor sounds like Tooter (a person who plays the horn)
6	KNIGHT	Knight sounds like Night (evening darkness)	5	TAILOR	Later is a Spoonerism of Tailor
9	MARSHAL	Marshal sounds like Martial (related to war)	7	HEROINE	Heroine sounds like Heroin (Drug)
11	BARD	Bard sounds like Barred (not allowed to enter)	8	PROPHET	Prophet sounds like Profit (Make money!)
14	PRINCIPAL	Principal sounds like Principle (fundamental truth)	10	SELLER	Seller sounds like Cellar (basement)
15	RAPPER	Rapper sounds like Wrapper (spoken word musician)	12	WITCH	Witch sounds like Which (Asking for specifying information)
16	FRIAR	Friar sounds like Fryer (broiler)	13	BEAU	Beau sounds like Bow (decorative knot)

HOMOPHONE REVIEW ONLY

Body Parts on pg 20

ACROSS			DOWN		
#	Answer	Explanation	#	Answer	Explanation
3	MOUTH	Mouth is an anagram of: Uh, Tom	1	NOSE	Nose sounds like Knows (is aware)
5	ANKLE	Ankle is hidden backwards: Pastel knapsacks	2	TEETH	Teeth is an anagram of: The E.T.
8	HIPS	Hips is hidden: Yeah, I psychotically	4	WAIST	Waist sounds like Waste (trash)
9	HEART	Heart is an anagram of: Earth	6	CHEST	Chest is hidden: cliche standards
11	TONGUE	Tongue is hidden: Futon guest	7	STOMACH	Stomach is an anagram of: shot Cam
13	HAIR	Hair sounds like Hare (Wild rabbit)	10	ARM	Arm is an anagram of: Ram
14	KNEE	Knee is hidden: Book needs	12	NAVEL	Navel sounds like Naval (related to the Navy)

Countries on pg 21

ACROSS			DOWN		
#	Answer	Explanation	#	Answer	Explanation
1	JAPAN	Japan is hidden backwards: kidnap a jaguar	1	JAMAICA	Jamaica is an anagram of: Acai jam
3	SYRIA	Syria is hidden backwards: Dairy store	2	PERU	Peru is an anagram of: pure
4	ROMANIA	Romania is an anagram of: aroma in	6	BELIZE	Belize is hidden: Rebel, I zest
5	CHINA	China is hidden: Glitch in atoms	8	EGYPT	Egypt is an anagram of: Type G
7	GREECE	Greece sounds like Grease (oily substance)	9	CYPRUS	Cyprus sounds like Cypress (evergreen tree)
10	KENYA	Kenya is hidden: broken yacht	10	KUWAIT	Woo Kate is a Spoonerism of Kuwait
12	EQUATORIAL GUINEA	Equatorial Guinea is an anagram of: Aga, our quiet alien	11	MALI	Mali sounds like Molly (Ringwald)

ADD/DELETE & ABBR. WORDS ONLY

Animals on pg 26

	ACROSS			DOWN	
#	**Answer**	**Explanation**	**#**	**Answer**	**Explanation**
2	COW	Cowl without the last letter COW - L = COW	1	SHEEP	Record=EP SHE + EP = SHEEP
5	LIZARD	Wife=W,50=L WIZARD - W + L = LIZARD	2	CHINCHILLA	INCH inside CHILL next to A CH<u>INCH</u>ILL<u>A</u>
6	BEAVER	A=A, Victory=V BEER + AV = BEAVER	3	FROG	River=R FOG + R = FROG
8	SLOTH	Hospital=H SLOT + H = SLOTH	4	WEASEL	Whiskey=W W + EASEL = WEASEL
10	CAMEL	Browned sugar=CARAMEL, Artillery=RA CARAMEL - RA = CAMEL	7	MONKEY	King=K K + MONEY = MONKEY
12	LLAMA	Los Angeles=LA LAM inside LA = LLAMA	9	BAT	Hot=H BATH - H = BAT
13	SEAL	Southeast=SE, Alabama=AL SE + AL = SEAL	11	EMU	Very loud=FF, Arkansas=AR, Soprano=S EARMUFFS - FF - AR - S = EMU

Round Things on pg 27

	ACROSS			DOWN	
#	**Answer**	**Explanation**	**#**	**Answer**	**Explanation**
4	FRISBEE	One=I, Small=S, Boy=B ISB inside FREE = FRISBEE	1	TORTILLA	Tango=T T + OR + TILL + A = TORTILLA
6	CLOCK	See=C C + LOCK = CLOCK	2	HUB	Senior=SR SHRUB - SR = HUB
7	SALAMI	South Africa=SA, Two notes=LA & MI SA + LA + MI = SALAMI	3	MELON	Maine=ME, Left=L, Nothing=O, New=N ME + L + O + N = MELON
8	BAGEL	The Spanish=EL BAG + EL = BAGEL	5	GONG	Iodine=I GOING - I = GONG
10	PEARL	Pressure=P P + EARL = PEARL	9	ACORN	Alpha=A A + CORN = ACORN
12	OLIVE	Four=IV OLE + IV = OLIVE	10	PENNY	New York=NY PEN + NY = PENNY
13	MOON	Right=R MORON - R = MOON	11	RINGS	Brings without the first letter BRINGS - R = RINGS

<u>ADD/DELETE & ABBR. REVIEW ONLY</u>

Things Found in Pockets on pg 28

ACROSS			DOWN		
#	Answer	Explanation	#	Answer	Explanation
4	PHONE	Page=P, Hospital=H P + H + ONE = PHONE	1	TOOTHPICK	Toothpick is an anagram of: Took pitch
5	CANDY	See=C C + ANDY = CANDY	2	CASH	Cash sounds like Cache (hidden storage)
6	KEY	Key is hidden: Pin<u>key</u>e	3	MEDICINE	Medicine is an anagram of: nice dime
8	LIGHTER	Lighter is hidden: twi<u>light, er</u>ased	7	WALLET	WET on the outside of ALL gives W<u>ALL</u>ET
12	DICE	A=A, Five=V ADVICE - AV = DICE	9	GUM	Gum is the reverse of Mug
13	LIP BALM	Lip balm is an anagram of: bill Pam	10	TRASH	Trash is hidden: ex<u>tra sh</u>ack
14	HANDKER-CHIEF	Handkerchief is an anagram of: Chef and hiker	11	RECEIPT	Receipt sounds like Reseat
15	FEATHER	Earth=E FATHER + E = FEATHER	14	HOLE	Hole sounds like Whole (total)

Bugs on pg 29

ACROSS			DOWN		
#	Answer	Explanation	#	Answer	Explanation
2	ANT	Pant without the first letter PANT - P = ANT	1	MOTH	November=N MONTH - N = MOTH
5	GRASSHOPPER	Grasshopper is an anagram of: rags he props	3	TSETSE	Tsetse is hidden: can'<u>t set se</u>rmon
6	APHID	Aphid is hidden: Gr<u>aph id</u>entified	4	BEETLE	Belgium=BE, Alien=ET, Left=L, Earth=E BE + ET + L + E = BEETLE
7	LOCUST	Locust is an anagram of: clouts	5	GNAT	Gnat is hidden backwards: <u>tang</u>
10	FLEA	Flea sounds like Flee (Run away)	8	CICADA	California=CA, Democrat=D CIA imprisons CAD = CICADA
11	PRAYING MANTIS	Praying mantis is an anagram of: spy marinating	9	SNAIL	New=N SAIL + N = SNAIL
13	LICE	I=I, See=C, the French=LE IC inside LE = LICE	12	TICK	Tick sounds like Tic (habitual movement)

<u>**B&P and LETTER SEQUENCE WORDS ONLY**</u>

Boys' Names on pg 32

ACROSS			DOWN		
#	Answer	Explanation	#	Answer	Explanation
1	BEN	Empty bottle (BE) Bit of nectarine (N) BE + N = BEN	1	BLAKE	Head of Branson (B) B + LAKE = BLAKE
3	ISAAC	Even letters of: rigs balance	2	MIKE	Clear out 'milkshake' enough to get 4 letters: remove middle 4 letters MI + KE = MIKE
4	STEVEN	Heart of Boston (ST) ST + EVEN = STEVEN	4	SEAN	Close to Spain (N) SEA + N = SEAN
7	ADAM	Edges of armed (AD) Edges of asylum (AM) AD + AM = ADAM	5	NICHOLAS	Remove last letters (tails) of: Niche of last
8	JACK	First letters (leads) of: Joe around clean kitchen	6	PAT	Odd letters of: plant
10	OLIVER	Center of gross (O) O + LIVER = OLIVER	8	JOHN	First letters (beginners) of: jump over harmony news
11	SAM	Regularly means every other letter of: smarmy	9	JOEY	A glimpse of elegant (E) JOY + E = JOEY

Girls' Names on pg 33

ACROSS			DOWN		
#	Answer	Explanation	#	Answer	Explanation
1	DIANA	First letters (heads) of: down interesting avenue near Amsterdam	1	DOLLY	Head of yak (Y) DOLL + Y = DOLLY
2	ELLEN	Remove first letters (heads off) of: Well, Ben	3	ESTHER	Drop of scotch (S) S + ETHER = ESTHER
6	TAMMY	Even letters of: Steal mummy	4	AMY	Heartless meany (MY) A + MY = AMY
9	HANNAH	Last letters (finally) of: crush tea down in aroma cloth	5	SANDRA	Borders of Russia (RA) SAND + RA = SANDRA
11	EVE	Middle of fever is the middle three letters: EVE	7	LAURA	Initially lovely (L) L + AURA = LAURA
12	CAROL	A bit of omelet (O) CARL + O = CAROL	8	LILY	First letters (firstly) of: lady, i love you
13	ANNA	Second letters (seconds) of: Can Uncle Andrew have	10	MAYA	Odd letters (evens out) of: meaty man

Instruments on pg 34

ACROSS			DOWN		
#	Answer	Explanation	#	Answer	Explanation
1	TIMPANI	One=I IMP + TAN + I = TIMPANI	1	TUBA	Last letters of: can't you scrub a
4	BANJO	Graduate=BA, New Jersey=NJ, Oscar=O BA + NJ + O = BANJO	2	LYRE	Lyre sounds like Liar (fibber)
5	HARMONICA	Harmonica is hidden: charm on Icarus	3	OBOE	Oboe is hidden backwards: Theo books
8	SNARE	Snare is an anagram of: earns	6	CONCERTINA	Concertina is an anagram of: into cancer
11	SITAR	Last letter of Israeli (I) STAR + I = SITAR	7	KEYBOARD	B chord is a Spoonerism of Keyboard
12	TRIANGLE	Triangle is an anagram of: Integral	9	LUTE	Even letters of: flauntier
13	ORGAN	Morgan without the first letter MORGAN - M = ORGAN	10	CELLO	Close to Toronto (O) CELL + O = CELLO

Alcohol on pg 35

ACROSS			DOWN		
#	Answer	Explanation	#	Answer	Explanation
2	ABSINTHE	Absinthe is an anagram of: Banish E.T.	1	CHAMPAGNE	Champagne is a Spoonerism of: Pam, Shane
5	ALE	Bit of egg (E) AL + E = ALE	2	AMARETTO	Tenor=T A + MARE + T + TO = AMARETTO
6	SAKE	Odd letters of: Slap knee	3	SHERRY	First letters of Rowdy Raccoon Yoga SHE + RRY = SHERRY
7	RUM	Rum is hidden: Other umbrella	4	CHIANTI	Chianti sounds like key on tea
9	BOURBON	Be=B, Bishop=B B + OUR + B + ON = BOURBON	8	MEAD	Mead is an anagram of: dame
12	WINE	Swine without the first letter SWINE - S = WINE	9	BRANDY	Most of Brando = BRAND, Club=Y BRAND + Y = BRANDY
13	VODKA	Vodka is hidden backwards: freak dove	10	BEER	Tail of bear (R) BEE + R = BEER
14	WHISKEY	Whiskey is an anagram of: Key wish	11	GIN	Gin is the center of the word Aging

RARER WORDPLAY CLUES ONLY

Birds on pg 38

ACROSS			DOWN		
#	Answer	Explanation	#	Answer	Explanation
2	SWALLOW	Consume also means SWALLOW	1	HUMMINGBIRD	Purr = Hum
4	DUCK	Dodge also means DUCK	2	STORK	The bird that delivers babies
8	BLUE-FOOTED BOOBY	BLUE-FOOTED BOOBY uses only letters found in: flute body	3	WHIPPOORWILL	Lash=WHIP, Unfortunate=POOR Bequest=WILL WHIP + POOR + WILL = WHIPPOORWILL
10	IBIS	First letters (Initially) of: inspiring bird in stream	5	DOVE	Plummeted also means DOVE
11	SPARROW	Fight twice = SPAR and ROW	6	PARTRIDGE	Semi=PART Backbone=RIDGE
13	ROADRUNNER	ROADRUNNER uses only letters found in: Rondeau	7	ALBATROSS	ALBATROSS uses only letters found in: Lost bra
15	OWL	Owl is at the heart of Prowler	9	PIGEON	Swine=PIG Age=EON
16	CHICKEN	Cowardly also means CHICKEN	12	PARROT	Average=PAR, Decay=ROT PAR + ROT = PARROT
17	ROBIN	ROBIN Williams is the voice of Aladdin	14	RAIL	Fence also means RAIL

Plants on pg 39

ACROSS			DOWN		
#	Answer	Explanation	#	Answer	Explanation
1	NIGHTSHADE	Evening=NIGHT & Blinds=SHADE	2	SANDALWOOD	SANDALWOOD uses only letters found in: Old swan
5	RUE	Regret also means RUE	3	BUTTERCUP	A BUTTER CUP is a container of fat
8	MORNING GLORY	MORNING GLORY uses only letters found in: No, my girl	4	FOXGLOVE	Handwear=GLOVE for a Vixen=FOX
11	SPRUCE	Tidy up also means SPRUCE	6	CARNATION	Vehicle=CAR, Country=NATION
13	ASH	ASH is created by burnt wood	7	IRIS	IRIS is also found in the eye
14	PALM	Center of hand also means PALM	9	IVY	Starting to inch (I) Sides of vinery (VY)
15	DOGWOOD	Follow=DOG, Golf club=WOOD	10	ORCHID	Brutish monster=ORC, Stashes=HID
16	WHEAT	WHATHENSEAT - ATHENS = WHEAT	12	ELDER	Not younger also means ELDER

<u>RARER WORDPLAY REVIEW ONLY</u>

Herbs & Spices on pg 40

ACROSS			DOWN		
#	Answer	Explanation	#	Answer	Explanation
3	CARDAMOM	Check the ID of = CARD A Parent = A MOM	1	SAFFRON	Saffron is an anagram of: for fans
7	CURRY	Gutted uplander (UR) CRY + UR = CURRY	2	SAGE	SAGE also means wise
8	GARLIC	Garlic is hidden: vine<u>gar lic</u>orice	4	OREGANO	Even letters of: coarser grains of
10	PEPPERMINT	Peppermint only uses letters found in: Print me	5	CLOVE	Charlie=C C + LOVE = CLOVE
11	ANISE	Pinches of (starting letters of) Aromatics Needed In Seasoning Everything	6	TURMERIC	Turmeric sounds like: tumor. Ick
13	TARRAGON	Tarragon is an anagram of: tan rag or	9	ROSEMARY	Two ladies = ROSE, MARY
14	BASIL	Basil is hidden backwards: Lisa B.	12	DILL	TREADMILLS - MASTER = DILL

Collective Animal Names on pg 41

ACROSS			DOWN		
#	Answer	Explanation	#	Answer	Explanation
6	CAULDRON	Cauldron is an anagram of: Loan curd	1	HOST	Host is an anagram of: Shot
7	NEST	4=IV INVEST - IV = NEST	2	MURDER	MURDER also means kill
10	CONVOCATION	Criminal=CON, Occupation=VOCATION	3	PRICKLE	Drop of ranch (R) PICKLE + R = PRICKLE
11	PARADE	Parade is hidden: <u>spar a dem</u>on	4	UNKINDNESS	Unkindness uses only letters found in: used ink
12	POD	Initial letters of: Pack of dolphins	5	FLOAT	Nothing=O FLAT + O = FLOAT
13	HERD	Herd sounds like: Heard	8	TOWER	Hauler of broken vehicles is a TOW-ER
15	FEVER	FEVER also means run a temperature	9	BARREL	Barrel is hidden backwards: Ta<u>ller rabb</u>it
16	PARLIAMENT	Parliament is an anagram of: mental pair	14	BED	Odd letters of: bread

5-Letter Words Pt1 on pg 43

ACROSS			DOWN		
#	Answer	Explanation	#	Answer	Explanation
1	LEPER	Leper is an anagram of: Repel	1	LEGIT	Actual=Legit & Run=Leg It
5	SCARE	Healed wound=SCAR, Energy=E SCAR + E = SCARE	2	PRANK	Park borders (PK) RAN + PK = PRANK
10	AGLOW	Silver=AG, Bass=LOW AG + LOW = AGLOW	3	RADON	Radon is hidden: Con<u>rad on</u>ly
11	IDIOM	Stupid person=IDIOT, Mike=M IDIOT - T + M = IDIOM	4	FLOSS	Odd letters of follow=FLO Nazis=SS FLO + SS = FLOSS
12	GLAND	A bit of gray (G), Ground=LAND G + LAND = GLAND	5	SWISS	Southwest=SW, One=I Possum heart (SS) SW + I + SS = SWISS
13	ICING	Icing sounds like: I sing	6	AMIGO	A=A, Note=MI, Half of goat (GO) A + MI + GO = AMIGO
14	OASIS	Love=O, A=A, Bro's sibling=SIS O + A + SIS = OASIS	7	EIGHT	Alien=ET, One=I, German=G, Husband=H ET + I + G + H = EIGHT
15	HEART	Hotel=H, Rate anagram=EART H + EART = HEART	8	CIGAR	See=C, I=I, Fish=GAR C + I + GAR = CIGAR
16	TOKEN	Hobbit author=TOLKIEN, Large=L Island=I TOLKIEN - L - I = TOKEN	9	EMPTY	Empty is an anagram of: my pet
17	SHORT	Missing=SHORT Brief=SHORT			

<u>EVERYTHING REVIEW</u>

5-Letter Words Pt 2 on pg 44

#	Answer	Explanation	#	Answer	Explanation
ACROSS			DOWN		
1	GOURD	Gourd sounds like Gored (pierced with sharp object)	1	GENRE	Genre is an anagram of: green
5	BROOM	Right=R, Loud noise=BOOM BOOM + R = BROOM	2	UPSET	Knock over=UPSET Trouble=UPSET
10	RUPEE	Redhead=R Final letters of Wide Awake (EE) R + UP + EE = RUPEE	3	DRYER	Doctor=DR DR + RYE = DRYER
11	OTTER	Pottery shell=PY POTTERY - PY = OTTER	4	SPARK	Spark is hidden: gro<u>ss park</u>ing
12	NOSEY	Singular=S, European=E, Club=Y NO + S + E + Y = NOSEY	5	BEARD	Grizzly=BEAR, 500=D BEAR + D = BEARD
13	ARIEL	Island=I Anagram of REAL = AREL AREL + I = ARIEL	6	OUIJA	Yes in French=OUI, Yes in German=JA OUI + JA = OUIJA
14	ERROR	Fish eggs=ROE, Falling back=EOR Railroad=RR EOR + RR = ERROR	7	MOLDY	Month=M, Whiskey finally (Y) M + OLD + Y = MOLDY
15	DENSE	Odd letters of doesn't = DEN Even letters of Usher = SE DEN + SE = DENSE	8	STINK	Stink is written backwards: <u>Knits</u>
16	ENTER	Center head (C) CENTER - C = ENTER	9	CRUEL	LUCIFER - IF = LUCER Cruel is an anagram of LUCER
17	DIARY	Help=AID, Returned=DIA Heartless Rodney (RY) DIA + RY = DIARY			

ACROSS			DOWN		
#	Answer	Explanation	#	Answer	Explanation
1	SUPER GLUE	Super glue is an anagram of: Reuse plug	1	SET	Southern=S, Alien=ET S + ET = SET
6	SIR	Yes in Spanish=SI, Republican=R SI + R = SIR	2	PERJURY	Judge=J, Old city=UR Youth originally (Y) PER + J + UR + Y = PERJURY
8	TORSO	Torso is an Spoonerism of: sore toe	3	RHOMBUS	Greek letter=RHO, Grand=M RHO + M + BUS = RHOMBUS
9	ALUMNUS	Alabama=AL, University=U Head master (M), Backwards SUN=NUS AL + U + M + NUS = ALUMNUS	4	LOATHE	Loathe is an anagram of: A hotel
10	THUMB	Husband=H, Male=M HM + TUB = THUMB	5	EQUAL	Eastern=E, Queen=Q Leads (first letters of) unusually artistic lifestyle (UAL)
11	HALFWAY	50%=HALF, (First letters of) works about yearly, HALF + WAY = HALFWAY	6	SINEW	Sinew sounds like: sin, you
13	USED	Used is half of the word conf_used_	7	RUSTY NAIL	CRUSTY SNAIL - CS = RUSTY NAIL
15	SHYEST	Quiet=SH, Heartless yeast (YEST) SH + YEST = SHYEST	10	TEST DRIVE	The heartless (TE), Saint=ST Desire=DRIVE TE + ST + DRIVE = TEST DRIVE
16	AMOEBA	Odd letters of armhole (AMOE) Degree=BA AMOE + BA = AMOEBA	12	ADAM	Barrier=DAM A + DAM = ADAM
19	AMMO	MOMMA - M = OMMA OMMA is AMMO backwards	14	STAR	Celebrity=STAR Mark=STAR
21	DECLARE	Declare is an anagram of: cleared	17	MONOCLE	Mike=M, Oscar=O Cleo mostly (CLE) M + O + NO + CLE = MONOCLE
24	NASAL	Nasal is an anagram of: Aslan	18	ENSURED	Ensured is an anagram of: end user
25	IGUANAS	South African=SA, Knight=N, Gold=AU, Soldier=GI SANAUGI is IGUANAS backwards	20	MESSES	Messes uses only letters found in: EMS
26	CORAL	Coral sounds like Choral: (composition made for choir)	22	CHUCK	Throw away=CHUCK Norris=CHUCK
28	ELK	Elk is hidden: Remod_el k_itchen	23	ANNOY	New=N, North=N, Duck=O, Why=Y A + N + N + O + Y = ANNOY
29	YESTERDAY	You archaically=YE Strayed anagram = STERDAY YE + STERDAY = YESTERDAY	27	LAY	Popular chip brand=LAYS Most of LAYS=LAY

ACROSS			DOWN		
#	**Answer**	**Explanation**	**#**	**Answer**	**Explanation**
1	EVAPORATE	Lay asphalt=PAVE, Westbound(reverse)=EVAP, Give a speech=ORATE EVAP + ORATE = EVAPORATE	1	EYE	Even letters of Retype (EYE)
6	FLU	Flu sounds like Flew (hovered)	2	ALBANIA	Virtually bans means BAN, Iowa=IA AL + BAN + IA = ALBANIA
8	ELBOW	The Spanish=EL, ship end=BOW EL + BOW = ELBOW	3	ONWARDS	Old=O, New=N, Hospital rooms=WARDS O + N + WARDS = ONWARDS
9	RHUBARB	Rhubarb is hidden: ma<u>r hub arb</u>itrarily	4	AORTAE	Aortae is an anagram of: ear to a
10	DONOR	New=N DOOR + N = DONOR	5	EQUIP	Electronic=E, Joke=QUIP E + QUIP = EQUIP
11	ASPIRIN	Drop of paint (P) Aspirin is an anagram of: Raisin + P	6	FLAIR	City=LA FIR + LA = FLAIR
13	DREW	Sketched and Interest both mean DREW	7	URBAN MYTH	Urban myth is an anagram of: Burn my hat
15	HEARSE	Listen=HEAR, Closer to ominous (S) Echo=E HEAR + S + E = HEARSE	10	DEHYDRATE	Dehydrate is an anagram of: Heat Ed dry
16	APATHY	Route=PATH, Unknown=Y A + PATH + Y = APATHY	12	SWAN	Southwest=SW, North America=NA Fixed up (reverse)=AN SW + AN = SWAN
19	LONE	Lone sounds like Loan (credit)	14	RELY	EARLY - A = ERLY Rely is an anagram of ERLY
21	DONKEYS	Wear=DON, Essentials=KEYS DON + KEYS = DONKEYS	17	PERFORM	Odd letters of poetry (PER), Grand=M PER + FOR + M = PERFORM
24	RANCH	BRANCH - B = RANCH	18	TONIGHT	Oven emptied (ON) TIGHT + ON = TONIGHT
25	ALL-STAR	Completely=ALL, Lead=STAR ALL + STAR = ALL-STAR	20	OSPREY	Windows=OS, Not predator=PREY OS + PREY = OSPREY
26	OUGHT	Tough leader (T) OUGH + T = OUGHT	22	NYLON	Lie non is a Spoonerism of NYLON
28	EON	Eon is an anagram of: one	23	EXTRA	Former lover=EX Returned (reverse) art=TRA EX + TRA = EXTRA
29	ASYMMETRY	Scrap of mold (M) Asymmetry is an anagram of: A mystery + M	27	TRY	Time=T, River=R, Variable=Y T + R + Y = TRY

<h1 style="text-align:center"><u>YOUR FIRST CRYPTIC</u></h1>
on pg 6 & 48

	ACROSS			DOWN	
#	Answer	Explanation	#	Answer	Explanation
1	FUEL	Odd letters of faux eel (FUEL)	1	FOG	Bewilder and Mist both mean FOG
3	STAGS	Sorority leader (S) S + TAGS = STAGS	2	LAWYER	Returned real=LAER, Wyoming=WY LAER + WY = LAWYER
6	GLOW	Exhausted general (GL) A cry of pain (OW) GL + OW = GLOW	3	SLIME	Small=S S + LIME = SLIME
8	INDEX	Popular=IN, Key=D, English=E, Coordinate=X IN + D + E + X = INDEX	4	AUDIO	Gold=AU God from Italy=DIO AU + DIO = AUDIO
9	YAM	Month=MAY Making a come back (reverse)=YAM	5	SIXTY	Nine Romans=IX, Pigpen=STY STY + IX = SIXTY
10	EBONY	Box of nuts originally (BON) Every case (EY) EY + BON = EBONY	7	LANE	Louisiana=LA, Nebraska=NE LA + NE = LANE
13	PEARL	Fruit=PEAR, Tulip core (L) PEAR + L = PEARL	11	BORDER	Border is hidden: Bo<u>b or Der</u>ek
16	OUR	Our sounds like Hour (Period of time)	12	NEST	Half of plainest is NEST
17	AGONY	ANY + GO = AGONY	13	POACH	Quiet=P, Oscar=O, Empty athletic (AC), Hospital=H P + O + AC + H = POACH
18	DATA	Data is an anagram of: Ta-da	14	ALOFT	Aloft is an anagram of: Float
20	HOTEL	Furious=HOT, The Spanish=EL HOT + EL = HOTEL	15	LOYAL	Loyal is hidden backwards: P<u>lay ol</u>d
21	ROLL	Bridge monster=TROLL, Tea=T TROLL - T = ROLL	19	ALL	Subtract first letter of mall (won't start) MALL - M = ALL

CONGRATS!

You've made it to the end! Hopefully at this point, you are more confident in your cryptic crossword skills.

To keep learning, these are some other avenues I recommend researching.

<u>Books to check out:</u>

Sutherland, Denise. *Cryptic Crosswords for Dummies*. John Wiley & Sons, 2012.

Moorey, Tim. *How to Crack Cryptic Crosswords*. HarperCollins Publishers, 2018.

<u>YouTube playlist of cryptic solvers:</u>

Cracking The Cryptic. *Cryptic Crossword: Beginner Guides.* Online video playlist. YouTube, 2018.

<u>Larger abbreviation list:</u>

Hall, Michael. "Cracking Crosswords." *Cracking Crosswords: Abbreviations*, 2022, http://www.crackingcrosswords.co.uk/abbreviations.html.

<u>Free cryptic games online:</u>

Miller, Darren. "Darren's Puzzles." *Search Results for Cryptic*, 16 Oct. 2022, https://darrenspuzzles.blogspot.com/search/?q=cryptic.

Lovatt, James and Christine. "Play Lovatts Free Online Cryptic Crossword - Updated Daily." *Lovatts Crossword Puzzles Games & Trivia*, 13 Sept. 2022, https://lovattspuzzles.com/online-puzzles-competitions/daily-cryptic-crossword/.

I'll also have other cryptic crossword related documents available on Etsy if you'd like to check those out!

Thanks for reading, and I hope this gives you a head start on your love for cryptic crosswords. :)